Workbook: Homework and Character Book
作業和寫字簿

to Accompany

Chinese Link
中 文 天 地

Zhōng Wén Tiān Dì

Intermediate Chinese

Level 2	Part 1

吳素美
Sue-mei Wu

于月明
Yueming Yu

張燕輝
Yanhui Zhang

Carnegie Mellon University

Upper Saddle River, New Jersey 07458

Acquisitions Editor: Rachel McCoy
Editorial Assistant: Alexei Soma
Director of Marketing: Kristine Suárez
Director of Editorial Development: Julia Caballero
Production Supervision: Nancy Stevenson
Project Manager: Margaret Chan, Graphicraft
Assistant Director of Production: Mary Rottino
Supplements Editor: Meriel Martínez
Senior Media Editor: Samantha Alducin
Prepress and Manufacturing Buyer: Brian Mackey
Prepress and Manufacturing Manager: Nick Sklitsis
Interior and Cover Design: Wanda España/Wee Design Group
Senior Marketing Manager: Denise E. Miller
Marketing Coordinator: William J. Bliss
Assistant Development Editor/Editorial Supervisor: Debbie King
Publisher: Phil Miller
Cover Image: Richard Nowitz Photography

This book was set in 12/15 Sabon by Graphicraft Ltd., Hong Kong, and was printed and bound by Bind-Rite Graphics, Inc. The cover was printed by Bind-Rite Graphics, Inc.

Printed in the United States of America
10 9 8 7 6 5 4 3

ISBN 0-13-224977-4
978-0-13-224977-5

Pearson Education LTD., *London*
Pearson Education Australia PTY, Limited, *Sydney*
Pearson Education Singapore Pte. Ltd
Pearson Education North Asia Ltd., *Hong Kong*
Pearson Education Canada, Ltd., *Toronto*
Pearson Educación de México, S.A. de C.V.
Pearson Education-Japan, *Tokyo*
Pearson Education Malaysia, Pte. Ltd
Pearson Education, *Upper Saddle River*, New Jersey

目錄 (目录) CONTENTS

Name: ____________ Date: ____________

Lesson 1 I Parked the Car on the Side
第一課 我把車停在旁邊 (第一课 我把车停在旁边)

I. Listening exercises

A. Listen to the dialogue, and then answer the questions below in Chinese:

New Word: 交 [jiāo]: to submit

1. 小紅在做什麼呢？為什麼 [wèishénme] (why)?
   小红在做什么呢？为什么 [wèishénme] (why)?

   ____

2. 小紅昨天晚上怎麼整理她的房間？
   小红昨天晚上怎么整理她的房间？

   ____

3. 明學要幫小紅做什麼？
   明学要帮小红做什么？

   ____

B. Listen to the dialogue and then answer the questions below:

1. 常天打電話給誰？他要做什麼？
   常天打电话给谁？他要做什么？

   ____

2. 他要搬什麼東西？搬到哪兒去？
   他要搬什么东西？搬到哪儿去？

   ____

3. 大概 [dàgài] (around) 要多少錢？
   大概 [dàgài] (around) 要多少钱？

   ____

II. Character exercises

A. For each character, make up two phrases, write the Pinyin pronunciation, and then compose a few sentences:

Example: 開(开):
開車(开车) [kāichē] 我會開車。(我会开车。)
開走(开走) [kāizǒu] 哥哥把我的車開走了。
(哥哥把我的车开走了。)

1. 撞(撞):

2. 破(破):

3. 累(累):

4. 整(整):

5. 壞(坏):

B. Write the traditional forms for the following simplified characters, then write the Pinyin pronunciation:

Example: 镜子 ___鏡子___ [jìngzi]

	Traditional Form	Pinyin		Traditional Form	Pinyin
1. 负责	______	______	2. 装坏	______	______
3. 房东	______	______	4. 大树	______	______
5. 挂好	______	______	6. 饿死	______	______
7. 扫地	______	______			

Name: ____________________ Date: ______________

III. Grammar exercises

A. Create a resultative complement, then write out a sentence.

Example: 到：找到　我找到我的書了。
到：找到　我找到我的书了。

1. 好(好)：

2. 上(上)：

3. 在(在)：

4. 開(开)：

5. 完(完)：

B. Change the following sentences into 把 construction sentences.

1. 爸爸穿上那件新外套了。
爸爸穿上那件新外套了。

____

2. 他要幫我裝好電腦。
他要帮我装好电脑。

____

3. 媽媽回來以後就打開門和窗戶。
妈妈回来以后就打开门和窗户。

____

4. 他寫错那個字了。
他写错那个字了。

____

5. 妹妹吃了我的蛋糕。
妹妹吃了我的蛋糕。

____

6. 弟弟打破鏡子了。
弟弟打破镜子了。

____

IV. Comprehensive exercises

小謝(小谢) was quite busy yesterday. This is his diary. Please translate it into Chinese characters. Pay attention to 把 and the resultative complement. (Use one character per blank).

1. I was busy to death yesterday. I did a lot of work and it has made me terribly tired.

昨天我 ______ ______ 了，我做了很多事，______ 我 ______ ______ 了。

昨天我 ______ ______ 了，我做了很多事，______ 我 ______ ______ 了。

2. My friends are coming over so I must clean up my house.

我朋友要 ______ ______ 看我，我得 ______ ______ 我的房子。

我朋友要 ______ ______ 看我，我得 ______ ______ 我的房子。

Name: ________________ Date: ____________

3. Cleaning my house was very tiring: I washed all the clothes and hung them up. I put all the books on the desk and the bookshelf. I also cleaned the carpet.

New Words: 擺(摆) [bǎi]: to place　　書架(书架) [shūjià]: bookshelf
吸(吸) [xī]: to suck　　地毯(地毯) [dìtǎn]: carpet
乾淨(干净) [gānjing]: clean

______ ______ 房子真 ______ 我 ______ ______ 了：我 ______ ______

______ ______ 了，______ ______，也 ______ 書都擺 ______ 書桌和書架

上。我還 ______ 地毯 ______ ______ ______ 了。

______ ______ 房子真 ______ 我 ______ ______ 了：我 ______ ______

______ ______ 了，______ ______，也 ______ 书都摆 ______ 书桌和书架

上。我还 ______ 地毯 ______ ______ ______ 了。

4. Finally, I also washed my car and parked it in the garage.

New Words: 最後(最后) [zuìhòu]: finally　　車庫(车库) [chēkù]: garage

最後，我也 ______ 車 ______ ______，停在車庫裡。

最后，我也 ______ 车 ______ ______，停在车库里。

5. My friends brought a cake over. I cut the cake into pieces with a knife.

New Words: 刀子(刀子) [dāozi]: knife　　切(切) [qiē]: to cut
塊(块) [kuài]: M.W. for chunk-like objects

我朋友 ______ ______ 了一個蛋糕。我用刀子 ______ 蛋糕 ______ 成幾塊。

我朋友 ______ ______ 了一个蛋糕。我用刀子 ______ 蛋糕 ______ 成几块。

6. Then we sat down and watched a movie.

然後我們 ______ ______ ______ 看電影。

然后我们 ______ ______ ______ 看电影。

7. That movie was so scary. It frightened me to death.

New Words: 部(部) [bù]: M.W. for movies
可怕(可怕) [kěpà]: scary
嚇(吓) [xià]: frighten

那部電影很可怕，______ 我 ______ ______ ______。

那部电影很可怕，______ 我 ______ ______ ______。

8. After finishing the movie, my friends said they were leaving.

______ ______ 電影以後，我朋友說他們要走了。

______ ______ 电影以后，我朋友说他们要走了。

9. It was very cold outside. They left without putting their hats on.

New Words: 戴(戴) [dài]: to put on (accessories)
帽子(帽子) [màozi]: hat

外面 ______ ______ 了，他們 ______ ______ ______ 帽子 ______ ______ 就走了。

外面 ______ ______ 了，他们 ______ ______ ______ 帽子 ______ ______ 就走了。

10. I felt cold, I put on my coat. Then I turned off the light, went to bed and slept.

我覺得很冷，我 ______ ______ ______ ______ ______。然後我把 ______
______ ______，上床睡覺了。

我觉得很冷，我 ______ ______ ______ ______ ______。然后我把 ______
______ ______，上床睡觉了。

Name: ________________ Date: ____________

Lesson 2 There Is a Picture Hanging on the Wall
第二課 牆上掛著一張照片 (第二课 墙上挂着一张照片)

I. Listening exercises

A. Listen, then mark the correct statements with "✔" and incorrect ones with "✗":

1. ( ) 桌上沒有小籠包。
   ( ) 桌上没有小笼包。

2. ( ) B 吃過餃子，也吃過小籠包。
   ( ) B 吃过饺子，也吃过小笼包。

3. ( ) A 說這家的小籠包很棒。
   ( ) A 说这家的小笼包很棒。

B. Listen, then answer the questions below in Chinese:

New Words:

附近(附近) [fùjìn]: nearby
蘇州(苏州) [Sūzhōu]: name of a town, Suzhou.
茶壺(茶壶) [cháhú]: teapot
一些(一些) [yìxiē]: some
姑娘(姑娘) [gūniang]: young lady
故事(故事) [gùshi]: story
有名(有名) [yǒumíng]: famous
彈詞(弹词) [Táncí]: storytelling performance
小城(小城) [xiǎochéng]: small town
特別(特别) [tèbié]: special
茶杯(茶杯) [chábēi]: tea cup
小吃(小吃) [xiǎochī]: snacks
唱(唱) [chàng]: to sing
告訴(告诉) [gàosu]: to tell

1. 他什麼時候去過蘇州?
   他什么时候去过苏州?

   ____

2. 他說蘇州怎麼樣?
   他说苏州怎么样?

   ____

3. 茶店的桌上擺著什麼?
茶店的桌上摆着什么?

____

4. 台上有什麼人，他們在做什麼?
台上有什么人，他们在做什么?

____

5. 他說那家店的茶怎麼樣?
他说那家店的茶怎么样?

____

II. Character exercises

A. For each character, make up two phrases, write the Pinyin pronunciation, and then compose two sentences.

Example: 開(开):
開車(开车) [kāichē] 我會開車。(我会开车。)
開走(开走) [kāizǒu] 哥哥把我的車開走了。
(哥哥把我的车开走了。)

1. 過(过):

2. 畫(画):

3. 拿(拿):

4. 裝(装):

5. 彈(弹):

Name: ______________ Date: ____________

B. Write the traditional forms for the following simplified characters, then write the Pinyin pronunciation:

Example: 镜子 ___鏡子___ [jìngzi]

	Traditional Form	Pinyin
1. 摆着	______	______
2. 各种	______	______
3. 乐器	______	______
4. 观众	______	______
5. 看过	______	______
6. 关公很神气	______	______

III. Grammar exercises

Translation:

明遠(明远) is reading an article about an Internet cafe in China. He would like to translate the following passages into Chinese to share with his Chinese friend.
(Pay attention to the usages of two 了(了); V. + 過(过); V. + 著(着))

1. He is an American. He has been living in China for three years. He has never been to an Internet cafe. This is his first time. (網吧(网吧) [wǎngbā]: Internet café, 網咖(网咖) [wǎngkā]: term used in Taiwan)

____

____

____

2. Inside the Internet cafe, the music is on. All the seats are full. Most of them are occupied by young people. (開(开) [kāi]: to turn on, 音樂(音乐) [yīnyuè]: music, 年輕人(年轻人) [niánqīngrén]: young people)

3. Some of them are standing; some are watching others play online games; some are sitting, writing e-mails and surfing the Internet. (別人(别人) [biérén]: other people, 線上遊戲(线上游戏) [xiànshàng yóuxì]: on-line game)

4. There are several servers in green shirts. They have big smiles on their faces. (掛著微笑(挂着微笑) [guà zhe wēixiào]: with smiles)

5. On the wall hang some advertisements for online games. Some high school students wearing school uniforms are looking at the advertisements and chatting. (廣告(广告) [guǎnggào]: advertisement; 制服(制服) [zhìfú]: uniform; 高中生(高中生) [gāozhōngshēng]: high school student; 聊天(聊天) [liáotiān]: to chat)

Name: ___________________ Date: _____________

IV. Comprehensive exercises

A. Read the following dialogue and then answer the questions in Chinese

繁體字:

家文: 你手上拿著的是什麼東西?

明華: 噢! 這是一本很有名的中國小說, 你看過嗎?

家文:《三國演義》, 我看過, 很不錯。我最喜歡關公的角色了。

明華: 我也是, 關公他畫著紅臉, 拿著大刀, 真神氣。

家文: 我也喜歡諸葛亮的角色。他常常拿著扇子, 彈著琴, 常常想出來很多很棒的計謀。

明華: 沒錯! 我也很喜歡他, 我很佩服他。

家文: 聽說《三國演義》已經拍成電視劇和電影了。你看過嗎?

明華: 我沒看過, 我們明天去圖書館借來看看, 怎麼樣?

家文: 好啊! 聽說還有《三國演義》的線上遊戲呢! 你玩過嗎?

明華: 我玩過, 很刺激, 很好玩! 現在我室友正在玩呢, 他已經玩了三個小時了。

家文: 我們明天一起上網玩玩看, 怎麼樣?

明華: 好呀! 明天借了電影以後, 我們一起上網玩玩看。

家文: 好, 一言為定!

简体字:

家文: 你手上拿着的是什么东西?

明华: 噢! 这是一本很有名的中国小说，你看过吗?

家文:《三国演义》，我看过，很不错。我最喜欢关公的角色了。

明华: 我也是，关公他画着红脸，拿着大刀，真神气。

家文: 我也喜欢诸葛亮的角色。他常常拿着扇子，弹着琴，常常出来很多很棒的计谋。

明华: 没错! 我也很喜欢他，我很佩服他。

家文: 听说《三国演义》已经拍成电视剧和电影了。你看过吗?

明华: 我没看过，我们明天去图书馆借来看看，怎么样?

家文: 好啊! 听说还有《三国演义》的线上游戏呢! 你玩过吗?

明华: 我玩过，很刺激，很好玩! 现在我室友正在玩呢，他已经玩了三个小时了。

家文: 我们明天一起上网玩玩看，怎么样?

明华: 好呀! 明天借了电影以后，我们一起上网玩玩看。

家文: 好，一言为定!

New Words:

有名(有名) [yǒumíng]: famous
角色(角色) [juésè]: role, character
諸葛亮(诸葛亮) [Zhūgě Liàng]: name of a person
扇子(扇子) [shànzi]: fan
計謀(计谋) [jìmóu]: plan
拍成(拍成) [pāichéng]: to shoot (become a movie)
電視劇(电视剧) [diànshì jù]: TV series
佩服(佩服) [pèifú]: to admire
線上遊戲(线上游戏) [xiànshàng yóuxì]: online game
刺激(刺激) [cìjī]: exciting

Name: ________________ Date: ____________

1. 他們在說什麼書？那本書怎麼樣？
他们在说什么书？那本书怎么样？

____

2. 他們都喜歡什麼角色？
他们都喜欢什么角色？

____

3. 明華說關公怎麼樣？
明华说关公怎么样？

____

4. 家文說諸葛亮怎麼樣？
家文说诸葛亮怎么样？

____

5. 他們約好要一起去圖書館做什麼？
他们约好要一起去图书馆做什么？

____

6. 明華玩過《三國演義》的線上遊戲嗎？他覺得怎麼樣？
明华玩过《三国演义》的线上游戏吗？他觉得怎么样？

____

B. Small essay: Describe something about your past experience. You may choose your own topic (such as an unforgettable event or person, most touching novel or movie, interesting game, party, or class, etc.).

New Words:

難忘(难忘) [nánwàng]: unforgettable
感動(感动) [gǎndòng]: touching

Requirements:

1. Apply the grammar points: two 了; V. + 過(过); V. + 著(着)
2. Compose at least 20 sentences.

Lesson 3 Go Straight from Here
第三課 從這兒往前走 (第三课 从这儿往前走)

I. Listening exercises

A. Listen and then mark the correct statements with "✔" and incorrect ones with "✗":

1. ( ) 這是火車站的廣播 [guǎngbō] (broadcast)。
   ( ) 这是火车站的广播。
2. ( ) 飛機再過十二分鐘就要降落了。
   ( ) 飞机再过十二分钟就要降落了。
3. ( ) 飛機就要降落在北京機場了。
   ( ) 飞机就要降落在北京机场了。
4. ( ) 這是中國航空公司的班機 [bānjī] (flight)。
   ( ) 这是中国航空公司的班机 [bānjī] (flight)。

B. Listen to the following dialogues and then answer the questions in Chinese.

Dialogue (1)

問題(问题):

1. 他要去哪兒?
   他要去哪儿?

   ____

2. 走路去要多久?
   走路去要多久?

   ____

3. 走到前面的交叉口，要往哪兒拐?
   走到前面的交叉口，要往哪儿拐?

   ____

4. 從那兒往前一直走，還要再過什麼，才能到呢?
   从那儿往前一直走，还要再过什么，才能到呢?

   ____

Dialogue (2)

問題(问题):

1. 旅客要去哪兒?
旅客要去哪儿?

____

2. 旅客以前去過上海嗎? 什麼時候?
旅客以前去过上海吗? 什么时候?

____

3. 那棟新大樓有多高?
那栋新大楼有多高?

____

4. 旅客以前常去小吃店吃什麼? 小吃店在哪條路上?
旅客以前常去小吃店吃什么? 小吃店在哪条路上?

____

5. 車費一共是多少錢?
车费一共是多少钱?

____

II. Character exercises

A. For each character, make up one phrase, write the Pinyin pronunciation, and then compose one sentence.

Example: 搭(搭):
搭公車(搭公车) [dā gōngchē] 我每天搭公車去學校。
(我每天搭公车去学校。)
搭乘(搭乘) [dāchéng] 謝謝搭乘中國航空。(谢谢搭乘中国航空。)

1. 降(降):

2. 向(向):

Name: ________________ Date: ____________

3. 繫(系):

4. 直(直):

5. 拐(拐):

B. Write the traditional forms for the following simplified characters, then write the Pinyin pronunciation.

Example: 安全带 安全帶 [ānquándài]

	Traditional Form	Pinyin
1. 农田	________	________
2. 拐几个弯儿	________	________
3. 系上	________	________
4. 后车箱	________	________
5. 人民币十块	________	________
6. 红绿灯	________	________

III. Grammar exercises

A. Answer the following questions according to your own personal situation:

1. 你住的地方離學校有多遠？走路要多久？
你住的地方离学校有多远？走路要多久？

____

2. 你有多高 [gāo] (tall)?
你有多高？

____

3. 你有多重 [zhòng] (heavy)?
你有多重?

____

4. 你每天背的背包有多重? 背包 [bēibāo] (backpack)
你每天背的背包有多重?

____

5. 你會開車嗎? 你開車有多快?
你会开车吗? 你开车有多快?

____

B. Translate the following into Chinese.

1. I cannot turn right here. It is a one-way street. I have to make a few more turns.

____

2. You go north from here, go to that intersection, then turn left.

____

3. I cannot recall his name.

____

4. He has been in a bad mood recently. He started smoking.
– 最近 [zuìjìn] (recently) 心情 [xīnqíng] (mood)

____

5. A lot of things are "to say it is easy; to do it is hard."
– 事情 [shìqing] (thing)

____

Name: ___________________ Date: _____________

IV. Comprehensive exercises

A. You have invited your friends to a party at your house. Now write an email to provide the time of the party, your address, and directions to your home. First draw a simple map of the directions.

Useful expressions:

往/向 + direction /location + V.; 拐, 轉(转); 離(离)……很近/遠(远)

Your map:

Your e-mail: e.g. time, place, direction, etc. (at least 12 sentences)

____

____

____

____

____

____

____

B. Write a short paragraph in Chinese (at least 15 sentences) to summarize the text. Try to use the following words and grammar points.

Grammar points:

往/向 + direction/location + V.; 離(离)…… 很近/遠(远);
(有)多 + Adjective (How Adjective?); V. + 起來(起来)

Words:

降落(降落)	搭乘(搭乘)	棟(栋)	旅館(旅馆)
拐(拐)	轉(转)	變化(变化)	農田(农田)
馬路(马路)	紅綠燈(红绿灯)	小吃店(小吃店)	
車費(车费)	人民幣(人民币)	找(找)	

Name: ____________ Date: ____________

Lesson 4 You Are the Same As Before
第四課 你們跟以前一樣 (第四课 你们跟以前一样)

I. Listening Exercises

A. Listen and then mark the correct statements with "✔" and incorrect ones with "✗":

New Words: 拜訪(拜访) [bàifǎng]: to visit

1. ( ) 他去拜訪了他的好朋友。
   ( ) 他去拜访了他的好朋友。

2. ( ) 老師和師母看起來都很健康。
   ( ) 老师和师母看起来都很健康。

3. ( ) 他帶了美國文學書、維生素和茶給他們。
   ( ) 他带了美国文学书、维生素和茶给他们。

4. ( ) 師母做了年糕、小籠包和餃子。
   ( ) 师母做了年糕、小笼包和饺子。

5. ( ) 菜都是老師做的,老師做的菜很好吃。
   ( ) 菜都是老师做的,老师做的菜很好吃。

B. Listen to the passage and then answer the questions in Chinese:

New Words:

選(选) [xuǎn]: to choose
當(当) [dāng]: to serve as, to be
帥(帅) [shuài]: handsome
成績(成绩) [chéngjì]: grades, academic performance
如果(如果) [rúguǒ]: if
那麼(那么) [nàme]: then

問題(问题):

1. 她有什麼問題?
   她有什么问题?

____

2. 小李和小王誰比較高，誰比較帥？
小李和小王谁比较高，谁比较帅？

3. 小李和小王誰學得比較好？鍛煉呢？
小李和小王谁学得比较好？锻炼呢？

4. 小李游泳游得怎麼樣？小王呢？
小李游泳游得怎么样？小王呢？

5. 明天他們要做什麼？
明天他们要做什么？

6. 如果小王做飯做得比小李好，那麼她要選誰？
如果小王做饭做得比小李好，那么她要选谁？

II. Character exercises

A. For each character, form two phrases, write the Pinyin pronunciation, and then compose two sentences.

Example: 健(健)：
健身房(健身房) [jiànshēnfáng] 我每天去健身房鍛煉。
(我每天去健身房锻炼。)
健康(健康) [jiànkāng] 祝你健康。(祝你健康。)

1. 差(差)：

2. 習(习)：

3. 自(自)：

Name: ________________ Date: ____________

4. 方(方):

5. 長(长):

B. Write the traditional forms for the following simplified characters, then write the pronunciation using Pinyin.

Example: 适应 ___適應___ [shìyìng]

	Traditional Form	Pinyin
1. 师母	________	________
2. 干杯	________	________
3. 便饭	________	________
4. 永远年轻	________	________
5. 长了这么大	________	________
6. 头发	________	________

III. Grammar exercises

A. Answer the following questions according to your own personal situation:

1. 你跟爸爸誰高?
   你跟爸爸谁高?

   ____

2. 你比媽媽重嗎?
   你比妈妈重吗?

   ____

3. 爸爸和媽媽誰比較會做飯?
   爸爸和妈妈谁比较会做饭?

   ____

4. 你覺得中文是不是一天比一天難?
   你觉得中文是不是一天比一天难?

   ____

5. 你現在說中文是不是一次比一次進步?
你现在说中文是不是一次比一次进步?

____

6. 你和你室友(或者最好的朋友)誰比較大? 誰每天起床起得比較早?
你和你室友(或者最好的朋友)谁比较大? 谁每天起床起得比较早?

____

IV. Comprehensive exercises

Write a short essay in Chinese (at least 25 sentences) about your hometown. You can compare the following aspects of your hometown to another city: weather, people, housing, environment, schools, stores, transportation, etc)

Useful words and expressions:

– Simple Comparison: A 像 B; A 像/跟/和 B 一樣; A 比 B; A (沒)有 B (這麼/那麼)
A 像 B; A 像/跟/和 B 一样; A 比 B; A (没)有 B (这么/那么)

– Comparison: Relative, Superlative and Emphatic degree 比較, 最, 更
比较, 最, 更

– 比 + ... 多了 (比 + ... 多了)

– 穿(穿) 戴(戴) 難得(难得) 特地(特地) 適應(适应) 街道(街道)
習慣(习惯) 地道(地道) 家常便飯(家常便饭) 相聚(相聚)
熱心(热心) 有朋自遠方來，不亦樂乎(有朋自远方来，不亦乐乎)

小鎮(小镇) [xiǎozhèn]: small town
人口(人口) [rénkǒu]: population
好客(好客) [hàokè]: hospitable
友好(友好) [yǒuhǎo]: friendly

____

____

____

____

____

____

Lesson 5 My Trip to China – Review
第五課 我的中國行–復習 (第五课 我的中国行–复习)

I. Listening exercises

A. Listen and then mark the correct statements with "✔" and incorrect ones with "✗":

New Words:

讓(让) [ràng]: to let
意外驚喜(意外惊喜) [yìwàijīngxǐ]: joyful surprise
躲(躲) [duǒ]: to hide
突然(突然) [tūrán]: suddenly
燈(灯) [dēng]: electric light
舉行(举行) [jǔxíng]: to hold (an event, e.g. party)

1. ( ) 小雪知道她的朋友們要給她過生日。
   ( ) 小雪知道她的朋友们要给她过生日。
2. ( ) 小雪跟夏華的弟弟都是21歲。
   ( ) 小雪跟夏华的弟弟都是21岁。
3. ( ) 生日舞會在星期六晚上舉行。
   ( ) 生日舞会在星期六晚上举行。
4. ( ) 小雪要去夏華的宿舍看電腦。
   ( ) 小雪要去夏华的宿舍看电脑。
5. ( ) 春紅帶小雪來的時候，她的朋友們都在客廳等著。
   ( ) 春红带小雪来的时候，她的朋友们都在客厅等着。

B. Listen to the telephone conversation and then answer the questions in Chinese.

New Words:
發(发) [fā]: to send
告訴(告诉) [gàosu]: to tell
沿(沿) [yán]: to go along
大概(大概) [dàgài]: probably

問題(问题):

1. 子英今天下午要去哪兒？
   子英今天下午要去哪儿？

   ____

2. 景文為什麼不能給子英發電子郵件？
   景文为什么不能给子英发电子邮件？

   ____

3. 景文要子英沿著第五大街往哪個方向走?
景文要子英沿着第五大街往哪个方向走?

4. 子英從第五大街往左拐以後一直走下去能看到什麼?
子英从第五大街往左拐以后一直走下去能看到什么?

5. 搭公共汽車去怎麼走?
搭公共汽车去怎么走?

6. 走路去要多久? 搭公共汽車呢?
走路去要多久? 搭公共汽车呢?

II. Character exercises

A. For each character, make up two phrases, write the Pinyin pronunciation, and then compose a few sentences.

Example: 班:

班機(班机) [bānjī] 我們的班機誤點了。(我们的班机误点了。)

暑期班(暑期班) [shǔqībān] 他申請了去上海的暑期班學習。(他申请了去上海的暑期班学习。)

1. 外(外):

2. 時(时):

3. 壞(坏):

4. 地(地):

5. 眼(眼):

Name: ______________ Date: ____________

B. Write the traditional forms for the following simplified characters, then write the pronunciation using Pinyin.

Example: 热情 ___熱情___ [rèqíng]

	Traditional Form	Pinyin		Traditional Form	Pinyin
1. 终于	________	________	2. 繁荣	________	________
3. 赶上	________	________	4. 大开眼界	________	________
5. 京剧团	________	________	6. 闹笑话	________	________

III. Grammar exercises

Your Chinese friend 小明 is going to fly to New York. Because this is his first time traveling in the U.S., please translate the missing information to complete a short note concerning check-in procedures at the airport.

New Words:

候機(候机) [hòujī]: to wait for a flight
登記處(登记处) [dēngjìchù]: registration place
證件(证件) [zhèngjiàn]: documentary proof
工作人員(工作人员) [gōngzuòrényuán]: staff
標簽(标签) [biāoqiān]: label
貼(贴) [tiē]: to stick
登機牌(登机牌) [dēngjīpái]: boarding pass
保存(保存) [bǎocún]: to take care of; keep
通過(通过) [tōngguò]: to pass
安全檢查(安全检查) [ānquán jiǎnchá]: security check
筆記本電腦(笔记本电脑) [bǐjìběn diànnǎo]: laptop; notebook computer
通道(通道) [tōngdào]: channel
脫(脱) [tuō]: to take off
電梯(电梯) [diàntī]: elevator
地鐵(地铁) [dìtiě]: subway

小明(小明)：

1. ______________________________

(You must arrive an hour earlier than the flight departure time.)

2. 到了機場候機大樓以後，先找到美國航空公司的登記處，
到了机场候机大楼以后，先找到美国航空公司的登记处，

____

(show your plane ticket and photo ID to the airport staff,)

____

(the staff will place a label on your package,)

____

(and will give you a boarding pass,)

____

(Please take care of your boarding pass.)

3. 你要帶著行李通過安全檢查通道。
你要带着行李通过安全检查通道。

____

(Before you walk toward the security checkpoint, you must take out your laptop,)

____

(take off your shoes and put them beside your luggage.)

____

(Sometimes you need to open your luggage for the staff to check.)

4. 過了安全檢查通道以後，你要帶著行李往前走。
过了安全检查通道以后，你要带着行李往前走。

____

(Turn right after passing the elevator, and the subway stop is right there.)

然後請你搭地鐵到美國航空公司的候機廳。
然后请你搭地铁到美国航空公司的候机厅。

Name: ____________ Date: ____________

IV. Comprehensive exercises

Your friends held a surprise birthday party for you on Friday night. Please write a short "thank you" email in Chinese (at least 25 sentences) to express your gratitude to your friends.

Useful words and expressions:

從來(沒)有 …… (這麼/那麼) [从来(没)有 …… (这么/那么)]
特地(特地)　高興(高兴)　比較(比较)，最(最)，更(更)
熱情(热情)　把(把)　往(往)

Name: ________________ Date: ____________

Lesson 6 I Am Going to the Bank to Open an Account
第六課 我要去銀行開一個帳戶
(第六课 我要去银行开一个账户)

I. Listening exercises

A. Listen to each of the dialogues and then select the right answer to each question:

1. 他們在說什麼? (他们在说什么?)
   a. 去銀行開帳戶的事 (去银行开账户的事)
   b. 去朋友開的銀行 (去朋友开的银行)
   c. 大華銀行的利息 (大华银行的利息)

2. A 想做什麼? (A 想做什么?)
   a. 換美金 (换美金)
   b. 申請有利息的支票帳戶 (申请有利息的支票账户)
   c. 申請沒有利息的支票帳戶 (申请没有利息的支票账户)

3. 他什麼時候能收到信用卡? (他什么时候能收到信用卡?)
   a. 兩天以後 (两天以后)
   b. 上個星期五 (上个星期五)
   c. 七天以前 (七天以前)

4. 他可以換多少人民幣? (他可以换多少人民币?)
   a. 五百元 (五百元)
   b. 八百元 (八百元)
   c. 四千元 (四千元)

II. Character exercises

A. Convert the following Pinyin dialogue to characters:

Měiqín: Xiǎohuá, nǐ shēnqǐng xìnyòngkǎ le ma?
Xiǎohuá: Shēnqǐng le, kěshì wǒ hái méiyǒu shōudào xìnyòngkǎ ne.
Měiqín: Nǐshì shénme shíhòu shēnqǐng de?
Xiǎohuá: Liǎngge xīngqī yǐqián.
Měiqín: Nà nǐ zěnme hái méiyǒu shōudào ne? Shìbushì nǐ tián biǎo tián cuò le?
Xiǎohuá: Bù zhīdào. Wǒ zài děng liǎngtiān ba.

B. List words or expressions that are related to the following:

1. 帳戶(账户) (at least eight items)

2. 美金(美金) (at least four items)

C. Put the linking word 那 in the appropriate blanks in the following dialogues:

1. A: 小琴，你看我開什麼樣的帳戶比較好?
小琴，你看我开什么样的账户比较好?

B: 儲蓄帳戶有利息，可是每個月只能開三張支票。
储蓄账户有利息，可是每个月只能开三张支票。

A: 我不需要開很多支票，就開一個有利息的支票帳戶吧。
我不需要开很多支票，就开一个有利息的支票账户吧。

2. A: 先生，你要存多少錢?
先生，你要存多少钱?

B: 我存三千元。
我存三千元。

A: 就請你填一下這張表吧。
就请你填一下这张表吧。

III. Grammar exercises

A. Use vocabulary from the following list to form one phrase of each type listed below (You may use each word more than once):

Name: ____________ Date: ____________

開 快 取 存 填 好 我 櫃台
开 快 取 存 填 好 我 柜台

地方 支票 單子 外幣 款 兑換 方便 帳戶
地方 支票 单子 外币 款 兑换 方便 账户

Juxtaposed phrases: ______________________

Endocentric phrases: ______________________

"Subj. + V." phrases: ______________________

"V. + Obj." phrases: ______________________

B. Based on the population numbers given below (in millions), fill in the table (to one decimal), then number the countries in descending order:

New Words:

百萬(百万) [bǎiwàn]: million　　千萬(千万) [qiānwàn]: 10 million

億(亿) [yì]: 100 million　　全世界(全世界) [quánshìjiè]: the whole world

全世界(全世界)：6,400

中國(中国)：1,360　美國(美国)：292　德國(德国)：82　日本(日本)：128

法國(法国)：63　英國(英国)：59　加拿大(加拿大)：32

Country	Ratio of population to world population	Percentage of world population
中國 (中国)		
美國 (美国)		
法國 (法国)		
英國 (英国)		
加拿大 (加拿大)		
日本 (日本)		
德國 (德国)		

Order:

1. ________ 2. ________ 3. ________ 4. ________

5. ________ 6. ________ 7. ________

C. Please translate the following sentences into Chinese. Use the pattern "Noun + 這兒/那兒(这儿/那儿)":

1. You may go to the banking machine (ATM) to withdraw money.

____

2. Please go to the bank clerk to get a credit card application form.

____

3. There are many people here at the counter waiting to exchange foreign currency.

____

IV. Comprehensive exercises

A. Look up the interest rates for various accounts at a few different banks, then . . .

1. make a table of the rates at different banks.
2. make comparisons between the banks.
3. select one that you would like to use for your accounts.
4. state why you have made that selection.

B. Write a short passage (at least 15 sentences) about one of your banking experiences.

____

____

____

____

____

____

____

____

Name: ________________ Date: ____________

Lesson 7 I Can't Find My Phone Book
第七課 我的電話簿找不到了 (第七课 我的电话簿找不到了)

I. Listening exercises

Listen to the dialogue and then answer the questions below:

1. 王華寒假要做什麼?
   王华寒假要做什么?

   ____

2. 他們要去哪幾個地方?
   他们要去哪几个地方?

   ____

3. 文英為什麼要去上海?
   文英为什么要去上海?

   ____

4. 王華打算怎麼從上海去北京?
   王华打算怎么从上海去北京?

   ____

5. 昆明是個什麼樣的地方?
   昆明是个什么样的地方?

   ____

II. Character exercises

A. Write the traditional forms of the following characters:

订	羡	亲	实	风
○	○	○	○	○
○	○	○	○	○

网	签	飞	办	证

B. Find words in the lesson that have the following radical components:

1. 艹 ______ ______
2. ⺮ ______ ______
3. 言 ______ ______
4. 方 ______ ______
5. 手 ______ ______
6. 刂 ______ ______

C. List as many words as you can from the lesson that are related to the following:

Example: 電話－電話簿，號碼
电话－电话簿，号码

1. 旅遊(旅游)：________________________________
2. 城市(城市)：________________________________

D. 小美(小美) is writing an email to her mother about her plans to go to China with her boyfriend 家文 during the winter vacation. Fill in the blanks below with 打算(打算), 原來(原来), 比如(比如), 聚聚(聚聚), 網站(网站), and 如果(如果):

(繁體字)

媽媽：

今年寒假我 ______ 跟家文去中國旅遊。你覺得好嗎？______ 去年我們就 ______ 去了，可是你要我去加州，所以沒有去中國。今年我們 ______ 多去一些地方，______ 上海，北京，杭州，西安，香港，昆明，______ 時間來得及，我們都想去看看。家文特別想去上海，______ 他在那兒學習中文學了兩個月，他很喜歡那個城市。他還想跟以前教他的老師 ______。我們已經查了好幾個 ______，還能買得到便宜的機票。其實你跟爸爸也應該去玩一玩。______ 你和爸爸也能去，那就太好了！我希望你們能去。

女兒 小美

二零零七年十月二十七日

(简体字)

妈妈:

今年寒假我 ______ 跟家文去中国旅游。你觉得好吗? ______ 去年我们就 ______ 去了，可是你要我去加州，所以没有去中国。今年我们 ______ 多去一些地方，______ 上海，北京，杭州，西安，香港，昆明，______ 时间来得及，我们都想去看看。家文特别想去上海，______ 他在那儿学习中文学了两个月，他很喜欢那个城市。他还想跟以前教他的老师 ______。我们已经查了好几个 ______，还能买得到便宜的机票。其实你跟爸爸也应该去玩一玩。______ 你和爸爸也能去，那就太好了！我希望你们能去。

女儿 小美

二零零七年十月二十七日

III. Grammar exercises

A. Fill in the blanks in 小琴(小琴)'s diary with potential complement constructions. After you complete the passage, write as many questions as you can, using a potential complement construction in each one:

New Words:

多雲(多云) [duōyún]: cloudy
感恩節(感恩节) [gǎn'ēnjié]: Thanksgiving
外公外婆(外公外婆) [wàigōng wàipó]: grandpa and grandma (on the mother's side)
經驗(经验) [jīngyàn]: experience

(繁體字)

十月十六日　　星期六　　多雲

今年感恩節，我要跟爸爸媽媽和妹妹一起去洛杉磯看我的外公外婆。他們家現在只有兩個人，住在一棟很大的房子裡，有很多房間，可以住 _____ 很多人。外公外婆年紀很大了，坐飛機很不方便，來 _____ 東部，所以我們常常去看他們。外婆很會做飯，每次都給我們做很多好吃的東西，有時候都吃 _____ 那麼多的東西。

前天媽媽要我上網查一下航空公司的票價，看看買 _____ 買 _____ 便宜一點的飛機票。我查了幾個網站，都很貴，一張票都要五百多元，媽媽說太貴了，買 _____。

我有一個朋友在旅行社工作。昨天我想給他打一個電話，問問他能不能訂 _____ 便宜一點的機票，可是我打了幾次電話都找 _____ 他。今天下午我要去找他，看看他幫 _____ 我幫 _____ 我。我想他很有經驗，我相信他能找 _____ 便宜的機票。

(简体字)

十月十六日　　星期六　　多云

今年感恩节，我要跟爸爸妈妈和妹妹一起去洛杉矶看我的外公外婆。他们家现在只有两个人，住在一栋很大的房子里，有很多房间，可以住 _____ 很多人。外公外婆年纪很大了，坐飞机很不方便，来 _____ 东部，所以我们常常去看他们。外婆很会做饭，每次都给我们做很多好吃的东西，有时候都吃 _____ 那么多的东西。

前天妈妈要我上网查一下航空公司的票价，看看买 _____ 买 _____ 便宜一点的飞机票。我查了几个网站，都很贵，一张票都要五百多元，妈妈说太贵了，买 _____。

我有一个朋友在旅行社工作。昨天我想给他打一个电话，问问他能不能订 _____ 便宜一点的机票，可是我打了几次电话都找 _____ 他。今天下午我要去找他，看看他帮 _____ 我帮 _____ 我。我想他很有经验，我相信他能找 _____ 便宜的机票。

____

____

____

____

____

____

B. Complete the following dialogue by adding 嗎(吗) or 呢(呢) in the blanks to soften the tone:

(繁體字)

高利文：小雲，你寒假有什麼計畫 _____?

季小雲：有。我要跟爸爸媽媽一起去佛羅里達 ([Fóluólǐdá]: Florida) 玩。

高利文：你們要去多長時間 _____?

季小雲：大概兩個星期吧。

高利文：你打算帶什麼中文書去 _____?

季小雲：不打算帶。我想好好地休息休息。

高利文：你們怎麼去 _____?

季小雲：我們坐飛機去。

(简体字)

高利文：小云，你寒假有什么计划 _____?

季小云：有。我要跟爸爸妈妈一起去佛罗里达 ([Fóluólǐdá]: Florida) 玩。

高利文：你们要去多长时间 _____?

季小云：大概两个星期吧。

高利文：你打算带什么中文书去 _____?

季小云：不打算带。我想好好地休息休息。

高利文：你们怎么去 _____?

季小云：我们坐飞机去。

IV. Comprehensive exercises

Browse online to find some information about cities in China. Select one city that you would like to go and visit. Describe why you want to go there and whether it is accessible by plane, or train or ship. Find the airline that offers the lowest airfare and then write an email to your best friend to suggest a trip there during the winter break:

1. Use the following words:

   網站(网站) 聽(听) 訂(订) 航空公司(航空公司)
   便宜(便宜) 風景(风景) 火車(火车) 地圖(地图) 辦(办)

2. Use potential complements.
3. Write at least 20 sentences.

____

____

____

____

____

____

____

____

Name: ________________ Date: ____________

Lesson 8 You Are Much Busier Than Before
第八課 你比以前忙得多 (第八课 你比以前忙得多)

I. Listening exercises

A. Listen to the following dialogue and then answer the questions below:

New Words:

漂亮(漂亮) [piàoliang]: pretty
減價(减价) [jiǎnjià]: on sale
雅虎(雅虎) [yǎhǔ]: Yahoo
網站(网站) [wǎngzhàn]: web site
價格(价格) [jiàgé]: price

1. 電話公司的手機減價以後比原來價格便宜多少錢?
电话公司的手机减价以后比原来价格便宜多少钱?

____

2. 常天的手機是在哪兒買的?
常天的手机是在哪儿买的?

____

3. 電話公司的手機和網上的手機哪個價格更便宜?
电话公司的手机和网上的手机哪个价格更便宜?

____

4. 小謝有沒有手機?
小谢有没有手机?

____

5. 為什麼小謝說常天現在不能給中國的朋友打電話?
为什么小谢说常天现在不能给中国的朋友打电话?

____

B. Listen and then write out what you hear in Chinese:

1. ____。

2. ____。

3. ____。

4. ____。

5. ____。

6. ____。

II. Character exercises

A. Circle the character with a different pronunciation from the others, then write out its Pinyin pronunciation:

1.	[行]李	銀[行]	飛[行]
	[行]李	银[行]	飞[行]
2.	[樂]器	可[樂]	有朋自遠方來，不亦[樂]乎？
	[乐]器	可[乐]	有朋自远方来，不亦[乐]乎？
3.	特[地]	[地]道	認真[地]工作
	特[地]	[地]道	认真[地]工作
4.	照[片]	功夫[片]	喜劇[片]
	照[片]	功夫[片]	喜剧[片]
5.	值[得]	[得]去機場接人	難[得]
	值[得]	[得]去机场接人	难[得]
6.	方[便]	[便]宜	家常[便]飯
	方[便]	[便]宜	家常[便]饭
7.	[好好]地學習	[好]客	[好]吃
	[好好]地学习	[好]客	[好]吃
8.	時[差]	[差]不多	游泳游得不[差]
	时[差]	[差]不多	游泳游得不[差]

9. 長短 長大 長城

长短 长大 长城

10. 適應 應該 應有盡有 [yīngyǒujìnyǒu]

(to have everything that one expects to find)

适应 应该 应有尽有

B. Write the traditional forms for the following simplified characters, then write the Pinyin pronunciation:

Example: 关于 ___關於___ [guānyú]

	Traditional Form	Pinyin		Traditional Form	Pinyin
1. 轻松	________	________	2. 情节	________	________
3. 导演	________	________	4. 描写	________	________
5. 场面	________	________	6. 兴趣	________	________

III. Grammar exercises

Fill in the blanks and then answer questions:

New Words:

金庸(金庸) [Jīn Yōng]: a novelist

天龍八部(天龙八部) [Tiānlóngbābù]: a novel by Jin, Yong

電視劇(电视剧) [diànshìjù]: TV series

著迷(着迷) [zháomí]: be addicted to

光碟(光碟) [guāngdié]: VCD

套(套) [tào]: set

一口氣(一口气) [yìkǒuqì]: in one breath

根據(根据) [gēnjù]: according to

改編(改编) [gǎibiān]: to adapt

笑傲江湖(笑傲江湖) [xiào'àojiānghú]: a novel by Jin, Yong

成年人(成年人) [chéngniánrén]: adult

童話(童话) [tónghuà]: fairy tale

拍攝(拍摄) [pāishè]: to shoot, take a picture

想像(想象) [xiǎngxiàng]: to imagine

總是(总是) [zǒngshì]: always

(繁體字)

小方：小文，你知道最近北京 ____ 金庸的小說《天龍八部》改編 ____ 電視劇了嗎？

小文：我知道。我的表妹 ____ 金庸小說非常 ____ ____，她已經 ____ 這部電視劇的光碟 ____ ____ ____ 了。上個星期她 ____ 這套光碟借給我，我一口氣 ____ 它 ____ ____ 了。

小方：怎麼樣？這部電視劇好看嗎？____ 另一部根據金庸小說改編的電視劇《笑傲江湖》____ ____ ____ 哪部 ____ ____ ____？

小文：我覺得這兩部電視劇都很好看。它們的導演都 ____ ____。可是《天龍八部》對感情方面的描寫 ____《笑傲江湖》____ ____ ____，特技效果也 ____ 以前的電視劇好 ____ ____。

小方：有人說電視劇 ____ ____ 小說好看，對嗎？

小文：對，小說 ____ 電視劇好看 ____ ____。我覺得金庸的小說是成年人的童話，電視能拍攝的場面 ____ 人們想像的場面要 ____ 十倍。童話裡的世界總是 ____ 我們電視裡看到的世界精彩。

(简体字)

小方：小文，你知道最近北京 ____ 金庸的小说《天龙八部》改编 ____ 电视剧了吗？

小文：我知道。我的表妹 ____ 金庸小说非常 ____ ____，她已经 ____ 这部电视剧的光碟 ____ ____ ____ 了。上个星期她 ____ 这套光碟借给我，我一口气 ____ 它 ____ ____ 了。

小方：怎么样？这部电视剧好看吗？____ 另一部根据金庸小说改编的电视剧《笑傲江湖》____ ____ ____ 哪部 ____ ____ ____？

Name: ________________ Date: ____________

小文：我觉得这两部电视剧都很好看。它们的导演都 ____ ____。可是《天龙八部》对感情方面的描写 ____《笑傲江湖》____ ____ ____，特技效果也 ____ 以前的电视剧好 ____ ____。

小方：有人说电视剧 ____ ____ 小说好看，对吗？

小文：对，小说 ____ 电视剧好看 ____ ____。我觉得金庸的小说是成年人的童话，电视能拍摄的场面 ____ 人们想像的场面要 ____ 十倍。童话里的世界总是 ____ 我们电视里看到的世界精彩。

問題(问题)：

1. 《天龍八部》和《笑傲江湖》這兩部小說都是誰寫的？兩部電視劇的導演是一個人嗎？
《天龙八部》和《笑傲江湖》这两部小说都是谁写的？两部电视剧的导演是一个人吗？

____

2. 誰買了一套《天龍八部》的光碟？
谁买了一套《天龙八部》的光碟？

____

3. 《天龍八部》和《笑傲江湖》哪部對感情方面的描寫多一些？
《天龙八部》和《笑傲江湖》哪部对感情方面的描写多一些？

____

4. 《天龍八部》的特技效果怎麼樣？
《天龙八部》的特技效果怎么样？

____

5. 為什麼小文說金庸的小說是成年人的童話？
为什么小文说金庸的小说是成年人的童话？

____

IV. Comprehensive exercises

Write a short paragraph in Chinese (at least 25 sentences) to introduce a Chinese movie you have watched, a Chinese novel you have read, or a Chinese computer game you have played. Try to compare the movie, novel, or computer game with a counterpart movie, novel, or computer game.

Grammar points:

A 比 B + degree complement;

A 比 B + Adj. + Quantifier

連……都/也…… (连……都/也……)，對(对)

Words:

主要演員(主要演员) 場面(场面) 情節(情节) 吸引(吸引) 關於(关于) 精彩(精彩) 同意(同意) 感情(感情) 描寫(描写) 客觀(客观) 有興趣(有兴趣) 而且(而且) 方面(方面) 效果(效果)

Name: ____________________ Date: ______________

Lesson 9 You Are Getting More and More Energetic
第九課 你越來越精神了 (第九课 你越来越精神了)

I. Listening exercises

A. 文英(文英) recently has lost quite a bit of weight. Her friends are all amazed by her success and have come to ask how she did it. She is telling her friends about her efforts to control her weight. Her friends have quite a few questions. Listen to what she says and then answer her friends' questions for her.

1. 你為什麼要減肥?
   你为什么要减肥?

   ____

2. 你覺得少吃飯是不是最好的減肥方法?
   你觉得少吃饭是不是最好的减肥方法?

   ____

3. 如果要減肥，除了控制飲食以外，還應該做什麼?
   如果要减肥，除了控制饮食以外，还应该做什么?

   ____

4. 我知道鍛煉很重要，可是我沒有時間，怎麼辦?
   我知道锻炼很重要，可是我没有时间，怎么办?

   ____

5. 你每天鍛煉多少時間? 效果怎麼樣?
   你每天锻炼多少时间? 效果怎么样?

   ____

II. Character exercises

A. Complete the following expressions and then write out the radical in each character:

For example: 鍛 煉 (釒, 火)

1. 鍛_____ (   ) 2. _____ 神 (   ) 3. 健_____ (   )

4. _____ 果 (   ) 5. 鐘_____ (   ) 6. 其_____ (   )

7. _____ 持 (   ) 8. _____ 活 (   ) 9. 苗_____ (   )

B. Group the following characters based on the number of components each has:

健(健) 房(房) 效(效) 越(越) 瘦(瘦) 最(最) 當(当) 更(更) 矮(矮)
靈(灵) 活(活) 苗(苗) 條(条) 總(总) 甜(甜) 體(体) 減(减) 肥(肥)

For example: ▢ 更

1. ________________
2.  ________________
3.  ________________
4.  ________________
5.  ________________
6.  ________________
7. ________________

C. Complete the following short dialogues. Use 怪不得(怪不得) in each of the sentences you add:

1. **A:** 我最近一直去健身房鍛煉。
我最近一直去健身房锻炼。
B: ________________________________。

2. **A:** 我這兩個星期太忙了。
我这两个星期太忙了。
B: ________________________________。

Name: ________________ Date: ____________

III. Grammar exercises

Translate the following sentences into Chinese using the "越來越(越来越)……" or "越(越)……越(越)……" pattern:

1. The more exercises you do, the more energetic you will become.

____

2. More and more people are going to China these days.

____

3. Nowadays, people are getting more and more interested in losing weight.

____

4. The less energetic you are, the more you need to control your diet.

____

IV. Comprehensive exercises

Write a report of at least 12 sentences about your plan to lose/control your weight. You need to include the following:

1. Why do you need to lose/control weight?
2. If you have tried before, was it successful?
3. What do you find is the best way to lose/control weight and why?
4. Use (but not limit yourself to) the following words and patterns

比(比), 效果(效果), 越來越(越来越)……, 看上去(看上去), 靈活(灵活), 太(太), 更(更), 嘴(嘴), 越(越)……越(越)……

____

____

____

____

____

____

Name: ________________ Date: ____________

Lesson 10 My Plan for the Winter Vacation – Review
第十課 我的寒假計畫–復習 (第十课 我的寒假计划–复习)

I. Listening exercises

文華(文华) and 家明(家明) are chatting about their plans for summer study in China. 文華(文华) wants to go to Beijing while 家明(家明) prefers to go to Shanghai. Listen to their conversation and then fill in the blanks in the following table with information you have learned from their conversation:

Useful words and expressions:

寬(宽) [kuān]: broad
先進(先进) [xiānjìn]: advanced
故宮(故宫) [Gùgōng]: the Forbidden city
溫度(温度) [wēndù]: temperature
低(低) [dī]: low
其實(其实) [qíshí]: actually

	北京(北京)	上海(上海)
人(人)		
生活(生活)		
天氣(天气)		
溫度(温度) [wēndù]: temperature		
大學(大学)		
馬路(马路)		
商店(商店)		
玩的地方(玩的地方)		
變化(变化)		
其它(其它) [qítā]: others		

II. Character exercises

A. Write the Pinyin pronunciation of the following characters and form a word or phrase with each character.

For example: 向(向) xiàng 向左走

	Pinyin	Phrase		Pinyin	Phrase
1. 向(向)	______	______	2. 及(及)	______	______
同(同)	______	______	友(友)	______	______
回(回)	______	______	又(又)	______	______
3. 句(句)	______	______	4. 跟(跟)	______	______
旬(旬)	______	______	根(根)	______	______
5. 受(受)	______	______	6. 曲(曲)	______	______
收(收)	______	______	而(而)	______	______
7. 載(载)	______	______	8. 據(据)	______	______
戴(戴)	______	______	劇(剧)	______	______

B. The following paragraph is written in simplified characters. Underline all the simplified characters (except proper names) and then write them as traditional ones.

我已经申请了去中国的签证，计划下个月去中国旅游。可是我

____

的飞机票还没有买到。现在买机票比较难，我今天还要上网查一下，

____

希望能找到不太贵的机票。明天我还要去银行换一些人民币。根据

____

今天的汇率，一元美金可以换七元九角八分人民币。

____

我还想去试试爬长城，做一个“好汉”。再去看一场电影，最好

是张艺谋导演的功夫片，因为它的电影场面很大。

我相信我一定会满载而归。

C. Compose sentences with the following words and expressions:

1. 計畫(计划) (as a noun) ____________________

   計畫(计划) (as a verb) ____________________

2. 根據(根据) ____________________

3. 接受(接受) ____________________

   收到(收到) ____________________

III. Grammar exercises

A. Make comparisons between two Chinese movies you have seen. Write 10 sentences that use the word 比:

____

____

____

____

____

____

____

____

____

____

B. Write a short paragraph of about 10 sentences to update your doctor about your physical situation over the past three months. Use the patterns 越(越)……越(越)…… and 越來越(越来越)…… Other patterns for comparison may also be needed.

C. You have a little brother who is seven years old. Using the "Verb + Potential complement" construction, write about 10 sentences to describe his abilities.

Name: ________________ Date: ____________

IV. Comprehensive exercises

Write about your plans for the winter vacation. Use at least 20 sentences, and include the following:

1. Your fitness plans (motivation, expected results, etc.)
2. Your travel plans and destination(s) and why.

The following grammar points should be used:

1. Percentage and proportion
2. Different types of phrases
3. 比 for comparison + degree of complement
4. 跟……(不) 一樣 [跟……(不) 一样]
5. 不如/不行(不如/不行)
6. 越來越(越来越)……

倒

dào: move backward
倒車(车)

rén 人(亻)
person

倒 倒 倒

倒 倒

亻 仫 倒 倒 倒

樹

shù: tree
把樹撞壞了。

mù 木
wood

樹 樹 樹

樹 树

木 杜 桔 桂 樹

树

shù: tree
把树撞坏了。

mù 木
wood

树 树 树

樹 树

木 权 树

Guide for Students

1) Character with its stroke order indicated by numbers

2) Pinyin pronunciation, grammatical usage, and example sentence or phrase

3) Traditional form of the character

4) Simplified form of the character

5) Stroke order illustrated by writing the character progressively

6) Radical of the character with its Pinyin pronunciation and meaning

7) Ghosted images for students to trace over

8) Dotted graph lines to aid students' practice

Note:

Detailed information is presented once for characters with no difference between traditional and simplified forms (e.g. 倒). For characters which have different traditional and simplified forms (including such subtle differences as different radicals or stroke order) detailed information will first be presented for the traditional character, and then for its simplified counterpart (e.g. 樹 and 树).

Name: ____________ Date: ____________

Lesson 1 I Parked the Car on the Side
第一課 我把車停在旁邊 (第一课 我把车停在旁边)

倒	dào: move backward 倒車(车)	rén 人(亻) person	倒	倒	倒
	倒 倒				
亻 伾 侄 倒 倒					

别	bié: don't 别撞壞(坏)了。	dāo 刀(刂) knife	别	别	别
	别 别				
口 另 别 别					

樹	shù: tree 把樹撞壞了。	mù 木 wood	樹	樹	樹
	樹 树				
木 朩 桔 樹 樹					

树		shù: tree 把树撞坏了。		mù 木 wood	树	树	树
		樹	树				
木	权	树					

撞		zhuàng: collide 撞壞(坏)		shǒu 手 (扌) hand	撞	撞	撞
		撞	撞				
扌	扩	揞	撞				

壞		huài: bad 撞壞		tǔ 土 earth	壞	壞	壞
		壞	坏				
土	坤	坤	坤	壞	壞	壞	

坏		huài: bad 撞坏		tǔ 土 earth	坏	坏	坏
		壞	坏				
土	圹	圷	圷	坏			

Name: ____________ Date: ____________

呀	ya: (indicating surprise) 對(对)呀！	kǒu 口 mouth	呀	呀	呀
	呀 呀				
口	口一	口二	呀	呀	

鏡	jìng: mirror 鏡子	jīn 金 metal	鏡	鏡	鏡
	鏡 镜				
金	金亠	鏳	鏡		

镜	jìng: mirror 镜子	jīn 金(钅) metal	镜	镜	镜
	鏡 镜				
𠂉	𠂉二	钅	钅亠	镨	镜	镜

破	pò: broken 打破	shí 石 stone	破	破	破
	破 破				
丆	石	石冖	石厂	石卜	破

合	hé: combine 分工合作	kǒu 口 mouth	合	合	合
	合 合				
人 亼 合					

主	zhǔ: (主意: idea) 主意	zhǔ 丶 segmentation symbol	主	主	主
	主 主				
亠 亠 丰 主					

負	fù: bear 負責	bèi 貝 shell	負	負	負
	負 负				
⺈ ⺈ 角 负 負 負					

负	fù: bear 负责	dāo 刀 (刂) knife	负	负	负
	負 负				
⺈ ⺈ 负 负 负					

Name: ____________ Date: ____________

責

zé: duty
負責

bèi 貝
shell

責 责

責

责

zé: duty
負责

bèi 貝 (贝)
shell

責 责

责

李

lǐ: (行李: luggage)
行李

mù 木
wood

李 李

李

裝

zhuāng: install; clothes
裝電腦

yī 衣 (衤)
clothing

裝 装

裝

裝	zhuāng: install; clothes 装电脑	yī 衣 (衤) clothing	裝	裝	裝
	裝	装			
丬 丬	壯	壯	壯	𧘝	裝

掃	sǎo: sweep 掃地	shǒu 手 (扌) hand	掃	掃	掃
	掃	扫			
扌	扌	扫	扫	掃	掃

扫	sǎo: sweep 扫地	shǒu 手 (扌) hand	扫	扫	扫
	掃	扫			
扌	扌	扫	扫		

整	zhěng: put in order (整理: tidy up) 整理	pū 攴 (攵) literacy	整	整	整
	整	整			
束	敕	敕	敕	整	整

Name: ____________________ Date: ______________

理	lǐ: put in order (整理: tidy up) 整理	yù 玉 (王) jade	理	理	理
	理 理				
王 玾 玾 理					

箱	xiāng: box, case 箱子	zhú 竹 (⺮) bamboo	箱	箱	箱
	箱 箱				
⺮ 笨 箱					

衣	yī: clothes 衣服	yī 衣 (衤) clothing	衣	衣	衣
	衣 衣				
亠 亠 衣 衣 衣					

掛	guà: hang 掛衣服	shǒu 手 (扌) hand	掛	掛	掛
	掛 挂				
扌 扗 挂 掛 掛					

挂

guà: hang
挂衣服

shǒu 手(扌)
hand

挂 挂 挂

掛 挂

扌 扗 挂

累

lèi: tired
累壞了。

mì 糸(纟)
silk

累 累 累

累 累

田 甲 里 罢 累

累

lèi: tired
累坏了。

tián 田
land

累 累 累

累 累

冂 田 甲 里 罢 罣 累 累

死

sǐ: dead
餓(饿)死了。

dǎi 歹
vicious

死 死 死

死 死

厂 歹 歹 歺 死

Name: ________________ Date: ____________

附	fù: be near (附近: nearby) 附近	fù 阜 (阝) hill	附	附	附
	附 附				
阝 阝 附					

忘	wàng: forget 别忘了。	xīn 心 (忄) heart	忘	忘	忘
	忘 忘				
丶 亠 亡 忘 忘					

窗	chuāng: window 門(门)窗	xué 穴 cave	窗	窗	窗
	窗 窗				
宀 穴 穸 穸 窗 窗 窗 窗					

套	tào: cover (外套: overcoat) 外套	dà 大 big	套	套	套
	套 套				
大 本 套 套 套					

咱 (stroke order 1–9)	zán: we (including both the speaker and the person/s spoken to) 咱們(们)	kǒu 口 mouth	咱	咱	咱
	咱 咱				

口 口 叮 叩 咱

Name: ________________ Date: ____________

Lesson 2 There Is a Picture Hanging on the Wall
第二課 牆上掛著一張照片 (第二课 墙上挂着一张照片)

牆	qiáng: wall 牆上	qiáng 爿 slit wood	牆	牆	牆
	牆 墙				
丬 爿 ... 牆 (stroke order)					

墙	qiáng: wall 墙上	tǔ 土 earth	墙	墙	墙
	牆 墙				
土 ... 墙 (stroke order)					

著	zhe: (a particle indicating an aspect) 掛著	cǎo 艸 (艹) grass	著	著	著
	著 着				
艹 芏 ... 著 (stroke order)					

着

zhe: (a particle indicating an aspect)
挂着

yáng 羊
sheep

着 着 着

著 着

丷 兰 差 着

照

zhào: take (pictures)
(照片: photograph)
照片

huǒ 火 (灬)
fire

照 照 照

照 照

日 日刀 昭 昭 照 照

片

piàn: thin piece
(照片: photograph)
照片

piàn 片
piece

片 片 片

片 片

丿 丿' 片 片

北

běi: north
北京

bǐ 匕
dagger

北 北 北

北 北

丨 丬 北 北

Name: ____________ Date: ____________

台

tái: stage, platform
舞台

kǒu 口
mouth

台 台 台

台 台

ㄥ ム 台

擺

bǎi: put, place
擺著樂器

shǒu 手(扌)
hand

擺 擺 擺

擺 摆

扌 扌罒 擺 擺 擺 擺

摆

bǎi: put, place
摆着乐器

shǒu 手(扌)
hand

摆 摆 摆

擺 摆

扌 扌罒 摆 摆

各

gè: each, every
各種(种)

kǒu 口
mouth

各 各 各

各 各

ノ ク 夂 各

種	zhǒng: kind, type 各種	hé 禾 grain	種	種	種
	種 种				
丿 禾	种 稙	稙 種	種		

种	zhǒng: kind, type 各种	hé 禾 grain	种	种	种
	種 种				
丿 禾	和 种				

器	qì: utensil, ware (樂(乐)器: musical instrument) 樂(乐)器	kǒ 口 mouth	器	器	器
	器 器				
口 吅	哭 哭	哭 器			

演	yǎn: perform, play 演員(员)	shuǐ 水(氵) water	演	演	演
	演 演				
氵 沪	浐 浐	湇 湇	演		

Name: ________________ Date: ____________

表	biǎo: (表演: perform, play) 表演	yī 衣 (衤) clothing	表	表	表
	表 表				
一	二	丰	主	表	

表	biǎo: (表演: perform, play) 表演	yī 一 one	表	表	表
	表 表				
二	丰	主	表	表	表

鼓	gǔ: drum 打鼓	gǔ 鼓 drum	鼓	鼓	鼓
	鼓 鼓				
士	吉	壴	壴	鼓	

拉	lā: play (certain musical instruments) 拉琴	shǒu 手 (扌) hand	拉	拉	拉
	拉 拉				
扌	扌	扌	拉		

胡		hú: barbarian (胡琴: two-stringed bowed instrument) 胡琴	ròu 肉 (月) meat	胡	胡	胡
		胡 胡				
十	古	胡				

琴		qín: a general name for stringed instruments 胡琴	yù 玉 (王) jade	琴	琴	琴
		琴 琴				
一	干	王	玨	珡	琹	琴

彈		tán: play (a musical instrument), pluck 彈奏	gōng 弓 bow	彈	彈	彈
		彈 弹				
㇆	弓	弓吅	弫	彃	彈	

弹		tán: play (a musical instrument), pluck 弹奏	gōng 弓 bow	弹	弹	弹
		彈 弹				
㇆	弓	弓丷	弓𫩏	弓亶	弹	

Name: ____________________ Date: ______________

奏	zòu: play (a musical instrument), pluck 彈(弹)奏	dà 大 big	奏	奏	奏
	奏 奏				
〓 丰 夫 奏					

己	jǐ: oneself (自己: oneself) 自己	jǐ 己 self	己	己	己
	己 己				
㇆ コ 己					

齣	chū: (M.W. for dramas) 一齣戲	chǐ 齒 tooth	齣	齣	齣
	齣 出				
止 齿 齿 齿 齒 齒 齣 齣					

出	chū: (M.W. for dramas) 一出戏	gǔn 丨 down stroke	出	出	出
	齣 出				
㇗ 凵 屮 出 出					

戲

xì: traditional Chinese opera
一齣戲

gē 戈
spear

戲 戲 戲

戲 戏

戏

xì: traditional Chinese opera
一出戏

gē 戈
spear

戏 戏 戏

戲 戏

畫

huà: draw, paint
畫著紅臉

tián 田
land

畫 畫 畫

畫 画

画

huà: draw, paint
画着红脸

kǎn 凵
hole

画 画 画

畫 画

Name: ____________ Date: ____________

臉

liǎn: face
紅臉

ròu 肉 (月)
meat

臉 脸

月 月̂ 肸 肣 脍 臉 臉

脸

liǎn: face
红脸

ròu 肉 (月)
meat

臉 脸

月 肸 肸 脍 脸

拿

ná: hold
拿著(着)大刀

shǒu 手 (扌)
hand

拿 拿

人 今 合 合 㑒 拿

刀

dāo: knife
大刀

dāo 刀 (刂)
knife

刀 刀

𠃌 刀

神	shén: spirit (神氣(气): vigorous) 神氣(气)	shì 示(礻) reveal	神	神	神
	神 神				
丶	㇇	礻	礻	神	

座	zuò: seat 座位	yǎn 广 shelter	座	座	座
	座 座				
丶	广	广	广	座	座

滿	mǎn: full 坐滿了。	shuǐ 水(氵) water	滿	滿	滿
	滿 滿				
氵	汁	洪	洪	满	滿

满	mǎn: full 坐满了。	shuǐ 水(氵) water	满	满	满
	满 满				
氵	氵	洪	洪	满	满

Name: ____________ Date: ____________

眾	zhòng: multitude 觀眾	mù 目 eye	眾	眾	眾
	眾 众				
冖	罒	罒	罒	罒	罒	眾

众	zhòng: multitude 观众	rén 人 (亻) person	众	众	众
	眾 众				
人	仌	众			

站	zhàn: stand 站著(着)	lì 立 stand	站	站	站
	站 站				
亠	亣	立	立卜	站	

長	cháng: long 長城	cháng 長 length	長	長	長
	長 长				
一	厂	上	𠤏	𠤏	長

长

3 1 2 4

cháng: long
长城

cháng 长
length

长 长 长

長 长

丿 𠂉 长 长

Name: ______________ Date: ______________

Lesson 3 Go Straight from Here
第三課 從這兒往前走 (第三课 从这儿往前走)

往	wǎng: to, towards 往前走	chì 彳 step	往	往	往

往 往

ノ	彳	彳'	彳˙	彳亠	往

降	jiàng: fall, lower 降落	fù 阜(阝) hill	降	降	降

降 降

了	阝	阝'	阝夕	阝夂	陊	陊	降

落	luò: drop, land 降落	cǎo 艸(艹) grass	落	落	落

落 落

艹	艹氵	莈	落

落	luò: drop, land 降落	cǎo 艸 (艹) grass	落	落	落
	落 落				
一 艹	艹 莎 落				

全	quán: whole; intact (安全: safe) 安全帶	rù 入 enter	全	全	全
	全 全				
入 全					

全	quán: whole; intact (安全: safe) 安全带	rén 人 (亻) person	全	全	全
	全 全				
人 今	仐 全				

繫	jì: fasten 繫上	mì 糸 (纟) silk	繫	繫	繫
	繫 系				
曰 車	軎 軗	毄 毄	繫		

Name: ________________ Date: ____________

系	jì: fasten 系上	mì 糸 (糹) silk	系	系	系
	繫 系				
一	幺	幺	幺	系	系

計	jì: count, calculate 計算	yán 言 word	計	計	計
	計 计				
亠	言	言	言一	計	

计	jì: count, calculate 计算	yán 言 (讠) word	计	计	计
	計 计				
丶	讠	讠一	计		

算	suàn: plan, calculate 計(计)算	zhú 竹 (⺮) bamboo	算	算	算
	算 算				
⺮	笞	笪	算	算	

品	pǐn: article, product 用品	kǒu 口 mouth	品	品	品
	品 品				
口 口 品					

搭	dā: take (a ship, plane, etc.) 搭乘	shǒu 手 (扌) hand	搭	搭	搭
	搭 搭				
扌 扌 扌 扌 搭					

搭	dā: take (a ship, plane, etc.) 搭乘	shǒu 手 (扌) hand	搭	搭	搭
	搭 搭				
扌 扌 扌 扌 搭					

乘	chéng: ride 搭乘	piě ㇒ left slanted stroke	乘	乘	乘
	乘 乘				
二 千 乖 乖 乖 乘 乘					

Name: ________________ Date: ____________

航	háng: navigate 航空	zhōu 舟 boat	航	航	航
	航 航				
丿	力	舟	舟	舟	舟	舟'	航

棟	dòng: (M.W. for buildings) 一棟樓	mù 木 wood	棟	棟	棟
	棟 栋				
木	木一	木	木	木	棟

栋	dòng: (M.W. for buildings) 一栋楼	mù 木 wood	栋	栋	栋
	棟 栋				
木	木一	木	木	栋

交	jiāo: (of places or periods of time) meet, join 交叉口	tóu 亠 cover	交	交	交
	交 交				
亠	六	六	交

叉 1 2 3

chā: cross
交叉口

yòu 又
right hand

叉 叉 叉 叉 叉

フ 又 叉

口 1 2 3

kǒu: mouth; entrance
交叉口

kǒu 口
mouth

口 口 口 口 口

丨 冂 口

左 1 2 3 4 5

zuǒ: left
往左拐

gōng 工
labor

左 左 左 左 左

一 ナ 㔫 左 左

拐 1 2 3 4 5 6 7 8

guǎi: turn
往左拐

shǒu 手 (扌)
hand

拐 拐 拐 拐 拐

扌 扣 拐 拐

Name: ____________________ Date: ______________

直	zhí: straight 一直	mù 目 eye	直	直	直

直	zhí: straight 一直	shí 十 ten	直	直	直

里	lǐ: (公里: kilometer)	lǐ 里 inner	里	里	里

展	zhǎn: open up 發(发)展	shī 尸 corpse	展	展	展

變	biàn: change 變化	yán 言 word	變	變	變
	變 變				
言	䜌	䜌	䜌	䜌	變

变	biàn: change 变化	tóu 亠 cover	变	变	变
	變 变				
亠	亣	亣	亦	变	

化	huà: change (變化: change) 變化	bǐ 匕 dagger	化	化	化
	化 化				
亻	亻'	化			

化	huà: change (变化: change) 变化	rén 人(亻) person	化	化	化
	化 化				
亻	亻'	化			

Name: ____________ Date: ____________

農

nóng: agriculture
農田

chén 辰
celestial bodies

農 农

冂 冃 甴 曲 曲 曲 農 農

农

nóng: agriculture
农田

zhǔ 丶
segmentation symbol

農 农

冖 ナ 农 农 农

田

tián: field
農(农)田

tián 田
land

田 田

冂 冃 田 田

成

chéng: become
變(变)成

gē 戈
spear

成 成

厂 万 成 成 成

喔	ō: (an interjection indicating sudden realization)	kǒu 口 mouth	喔	喔	喔
	喔 喔				
口 叩	喔 喔				

尺	chǐ: ruler (公尺: meter)	shī 尸 corpse	尺	尺	尺
	尺 尺				
㇆ コ	尸 尺				

山	shān: mountain 黃(黄)山	shān 山 mountain	山	山	山
	山 山				
丨 山	山				

燈	dēng: light, lamp 紅綠燈	huǒ 火 fire	燈	燈	燈
	燈 灯				
丷 火	灯 灯	炇 炇	焂 燈		

Name: ______________ Date: ______________

灯	dēng: light, lamp 红绿灯	huǒ 火 fire	灯	灯	灯
	燈	灯			
丶	丷	火	火一	灯	

向	xiàng: to, toward 向右轉(转)	kǒu 口 mouth	向	向	向
	向	向			
丿	丿	冂	向		

右	yòu: right 向右轉(转)	kǒu 口 mouth	右	右	右
	右	右			
一	ナ	右			

轉	zhuǎn: turn 向右轉	chē 車 vehicle	轉	轉	轉
	轉	转			
一	戸	車	軻	軸	轉

转	zhuǎn: turn 向右转	chē 車 (车) vehicle	转	转	转
	轉 转				
一	𠂉	车	车	车ニ	转	转

彎	wān: curve 拐彎兒	gōng 弓 bow	彎	彎	彎
	彎 弯				
言	結	䜌	䜌	彎	彎

弯	wān: curve 拐弯儿	gōng 弓 bow	弯	弯	弯
	彎 弯				
亠	亣	亦	亦	弯	弯

費	fèi: cost, expenditure 車費	bèi 貝 shell	費	費	費
	費 费				
一	コ	弓	弗	弗	費	費

Name: ____________ Date: ____________

費	fèi: cost, expenditure 车费	bèi 貝(贝) shell	费	费	费
	費 费				
㇇	彐	弓	弗	弗	费 费

民	mín: people 人民	shì 氏 surname	民	民	民
	民 民				

民	mín: people 人民	yǐ 乙 second	民	民	民
	民 民				

幣	bì: money, currency 人民幣	jīn 巾 napkin	幣	幣	幣
	幣 币				

币 (stroke order 1–4)	bì: money, currency 人民币	jīn 巾 napkin	币	币	币
	幣	币			
一	丆	丙	币		

Name: ________________ Date: ______________

Lesson 4 You Are the Same As Before
第四課 你們跟以前一樣 (第四课 你们跟以前一样)

母	mǔ: mother 師(师)母	mǔ 母 mother	母	母	母
	母 母				
𠃋 ⺟ ⺟ 毋 母					

維	wéi: maintain (維生素: vitamin) 維生素	mì 糸(糹) silk	維	維	維
	維 维				
幺 幺 糸 糹 紃 絣 維 維					

维	wéi: maintain (维生素: vitamin) 维生素	mì 糸(纟) silk	维	维	维
	維 维				
ㄥ 纟 纟 纠 纠 维 维 维					

素	sù: basic element 維(维)生素	mì 系(糹) silk	素	素	素
	素 素				
二 丰	龶 丰 ... 素				

永	yǒng: forever 永遠(远)	shuǐ 水(氵) water	永	永	永
	永 永				
丶 亅	刁 氶 永				

康	kāng: healthy 健康	yǎn 广 shelter	康	康	康
	康 康				
亠 广	广 庐 庚 庚 康 康				

輕	qīng: small in degree 年輕	chē 車 vehicle	輕	輕	輕
	輕 轻				
車 車	軻 輕 輕 輕 輕				

Name: ______________ Date: ______________

轻	qīng: small in degree 年轻	chē 車 (车) vehicle	轻	轻	轻
	輕 轻				
一 ㄊ	车 车	轩 轻			

特	tè: specially 特地	niú 牛 (牜) cattle	特	特	特
	特 特				
㇀ 牛	牛 牡	特			

涼	liáng: cool, cold 菜要涼了。	shuǐ 水 (氵) water	涼	涼	涼
	涼 凉				
氵 氵亠	湇 涼				

凉	liáng: cool, cold 菜要凉了。	bīng 冫 ice	凉	凉	凉
	涼 凉				
冫 冫亠	冶 凉				

精	jīng: energy, spirit 精神	mǐ 米 rice	精	精	精
精 精					
丷 丷	䒑 半 米 𥸦 精 精				

髮	fà: hair 頭髮	biāo 髟 (of hair) dropping	髮	髮	髮
髮 发					
𠂆 镸	長 髟 髮 髮 髮 髮				

发	fà: hair 头发	yòu 又 right hand	发	发	发
髮 发					
𠃋 ナ	㔾 发 发				

眼	yǎn: eye 眼睛	mù 目 eye	眼	眼	眼
眼 眼					
目	目 目 目 目 眼				

Name: ________________ Date: ____________

睛	jīng: eyeball 眼睛	mù 目 eye	睛	睛	睛
	睛 睛				
目 目 目 目 睛 睛					

花	huā: (of eyes) blurred 眼花	cǎo 艸 (艹) grass	花	花	花
	花 花				
艹 艹 艹 花					

花	huā: (of eyes) blurred 眼花	cǎo 艸 (艹) grass	花	花	花
	花 花				
艹 艹 艹 花					

適	shì: fit, suitable 適應	chuò 辵 (辶) motion	適	適	適
	適 适				
亠 亠 产 啇 啇 啇 適 適					

适	shì: fit, suitable 适应	chuò 辵(辶) motion	适	适	适
	適 适				
二	千	舌	𠀉舌	话	适

差	chāi: errand, job 出差	gōng 工 labor	差	差	差
	差 差				
丷	䒑	羊	𦍌	差	差	差	差

差	chāi: errand, job 出差	gōng 工 labor	差	差	差
	差 差				
丷	䒑	羊	差

睏	kùn: sleepy 覺得很睏	mù 目 eye	睏	睏	睏
	睏 困				
目	目	目冂	睏	睏

Name: ____________ Date: ____________

困	kùn: sleepy 觉得很困	wéi 口 enclosure	困	困	困
丨 冂 闲 困					

街	jiē: street 街道	xíng 行 road	街	街	街
彳 彳 徍 徍 街					

街	jiē: street 街道	chì 彳 step	街	街	街
彳 彳 徍 徍 街					

慣	guàn: be in the habit of 習慣	xīn 心 (忄) heart	慣	慣	慣
丨 忄 忄 忄 忄 慣 慣					

慣	guàn: be in the habit of 习惯	xīn 心 (忄) heart	惯	惯	惯
	慣 惯				
丨 忄 忄ㄴ 忄口 忄罒 忄毌 惯 惯					

味	wèi: taste 味道	kǒu 口 mouth	味	味	味
	味 味				
口 口二 吁 呋 味					

香	xiāng: aroma, good smell 色香味俱全	xiāng 香 fragrant	香	香	香
	香 香				
丿 禾 香					

俱	jù: all, completely 色香味俱全	rén 人 (亻) person	俱	俱	俱
	俱 俱				
亻 但 侣 俱 俱					

Name: ____________ Date: ____________

飽	bǎo: be full 吃飽了	shí 食 (飠) food	飽	飽	飽

飽 饱

丿 今 飠 飠 飠 飠 飽 飽

饱	bǎo: be full 吃饱了	shí 食 (饣) food	饱	饱	饱

飽 饱

丿 饣 饣 饣 饱

便	biàn: convenient 家常便飯(饭)	rén 人 (亻) person	便	便	便

便 便

亻 亻 便 便 便

相	xiāng: mutually 相聚	mù 目 eye	相	相	相

相 相

木 机 相

聚	jù: gather 相聚	ěr 耳 ear	聚	聚	聚
	聚 聚				
耳 取	取 取	聚 聚	聚		

聚	jù: gather 相聚	ěr 耳 ear	聚	聚	聚
	聚 聚				
耳 耳	取 取	聚 聚	聚 聚		

乾	gān: dry; empty 乾杯	yǐ 乙 second	乾	乾	乾
	乾 干				
十 古	卓 乾	乾			

干	gān: dry; empty 干杯	yī 一 one	干	干	干
	乾 干				
一 二	干				

Name: ____________ Date: ____________

亦 (strokes 1–6)	yì: also 不亦樂(乐)乎	tóu 亠 cover	亦	亦	亦
	亦 亦				
亠 亣 亣 亦 亦					

乎 (strokes 1–5)	hū: (a particle expressing doubt or conjecture) 不亦樂(乐)乎	piě ㇒ left slanted stroke	乎	乎	乎
	乎 乎				
㇒ ⺍ 丘 乎					

Name: ______________ Date: __________

Lesson 5 My Trip to China – Review
第五課 我的中國行–復習 (第五课 我的中国行–复习)

陰	yīn: overcast 陰雨	fù 阜(阝) hill	陰	陰	陰
	陰 阴				

阝	阝	阝	阾	陰	陰	陰	陰		

阴	yīn: overcast 阴雨	fù 阜(阝) hill	阴	阴	阴
	陰 阴				

了	阝	阴							

終	zhōng: end (終於: at last) 終於	mì 糸(糹) silk	終	終	終
	終 终				

幺	糹	約	終	終	終				

终	zhōng: end (终于: at last) 终于	mì 糸 (纟) silk	终	终	终
	終 终				
𠂉 纟 纟 终 终					

於	yú: (終於: at last) 終於	fāng 方 square	於	於	於
	於 于				
亠 方 方 扵 扵 於					

于	yú: (终于: at last) 终于	yī 一 one	于	于	于
	於 于				
一 二 于					

誤	wù: miss 誤點	yán 言 word	誤	誤	誤
	誤 误				
言 訁 訁口 誤 誤 誤					

Name: ____________________ Date: ______________

误 (stroke order 1–9)	wù: miss 误点	yán 言(讠) word	误	误	误
	誤	误			
讠	讠口	误	误		

趕 (stroke order 1–14)	gǎn: catch, take 趕上	zǒu 走 walk	趕	趕	趕
	趕	赶			
土	丰	走	起	趕	趕

赶 (stroke order 1–10)	gǎn: catch, take 赶上	zǒu 走 walk	赶	赶	赶
	趕	赶			
土	丰	丰	走	走	赶

情 (stroke order 1–11)	qíng: affection 熱(热)情	xīn 心(忄) heart	情	情	情
	情	情			
忄	忄丰	忄丰	情	情	

津	jīn: saliva 津津有味	shuǐ 水 (氵) water	津	津	津
	津 津				
氵 氵 氵 氵 津					

界	jiè: boundary 眼界	tián 田 land	界	界	界
	界 界				
田 田 田 田 界					

團	tuán: group 劇團	wéi 口 enclosure	團	團	團
	團 团				
丨 冂 冂 冂 冂 冂 冂 團 團					

团	tuán: group 剧团	wéi 口 enclosure	团	团	团
	團 团				
丨 冂 团 团					

Name: ____________ Date: ____________

鬧	nào: do, make 鬧笑話	dòu 鬥 contest	鬧	鬧	鬧
	鬧 闹				
丨 ⺁ ⺁ ...	鬥 鬧				

闹	nào: do, make 闹笑话	mén 門(门) door	闹	闹	闹
	鬧 闹				
丶 门 闹					

笑	xiào: laugh 笑話(话)	zhú 竹(⺮) bamboo	笑	笑	笑
	笑 笑				
竺 笑					

繁	fán: numerous (繁榮(荣): flourshing) 繁榮(荣)	mì 糸(纟) silk	繁	繁	繁
	繁 繁				
每 敏 繁					

榮	róng: glory (繁榮: flourshing) 繁榮	mù 木 wood	榮	榮	榮
	榮 榮				
丷 火	炏 𤇾 𤇾 𤇾 榮				

荣	róng: glory (繁荣: flourshing) 繁荣	cǎo 艸 (艹) grass	荣	荣	荣
	榮 荣				
艹 艹	荣				

廈	shà: tall building 大廈	yǎn 广 shelter	廈	廈	廈
	廈 厦				
广 广	广 广 广 广 廈				

厦	shà: tall building 大厦	hàn 厂 shelter	厦	厦	厦
	廈 厦				
厂 厂	厂 厂 厂 厦				

Name: ____________ Date: ____________

雖	suī: although 雖然	zhuī 隹 bird tail	雖	雖	雖
	雖 虽				

口 吕 吊 虽 虽' 虽' 虽' 雖

虽	suī: although 虽然	kǒu 口 mouth	虽	虽	虽
	雖 虽				

口 吕 吊 虽 虽

挺	tǐng: very, quite 挺棒的	shǒu 手 (扌) hand	挺	挺	挺
	挺 挺				

扌 扌 扌 挺 挺

值	zhí: be worth 值得	rén 人 (亻) person	值	值	值
	值 值				

亻 亻 仿 值 值

Name: ____________________ Date: ______________

Lesson 6 I Am Going to the Bank to Open an Account

第六課 我要去銀行開一個帳戶

(第六课 我要去银行开一个账户)

銀	yín: silver 銀行	jīn 金 metal	銀	銀	銀
	銀	银			
金	釒	釒	鉀	鉀	銀

银	yín: silver 银行	jīn 金 (钅) metal	银	银	银
	銀	银			
𠂉	𠂉	钅	钅	钾	银

帳	zhàng: account 帳戶	jīn 巾 napkin	帳	帳	帳
	帳	账			
冂	巾	巾	巾	巾	帳

账	zhàng: account 账户	bèi 貝(贝) shell	账	账	账
	帳 账				
丨 冂 贝 贝 贝 贝 账 账					

戶	hù: door; (bank) account 帳戶	hù 戶 door	戶	戶	戶
	戶 户				
ノ 厂 户 戶					

户	hù: door; (bank) account 帐户	hù 户 door	户	户	户
	戶 户				
丶 ㇇ 彐 户					

存	cún: deposit 存款	zǐ 子 child	存	存	存
	存 存				
一 ナ 𠂇 存 存 存					

Name: ____________ Date: ____________

款

kuǎn: a sum of money
存款

qiàn 欠
owe

士 訁 訁 訁 款 款 款

取

qǔ: take, fetch
取款

yòu 又
right hand

丆 丌 耳 耳 取

利

lì: profit, interest
利率

dāo 刀 (刂)
knife

二 千 禾 禾 利

率

lǜ: rate
利率

xuán 玄
black

亠 玄 玄 玄 玄 率 率

率	lǜ: rate 利率	tóu 亠 cover	率	率	率
	率 率				
亠 玄	泫 泫	率			

儲	chǔ: store up 儲蓄	rén 人(亻) person	儲	儲	儲
	儲 储				
亻 信	佶 偖	儲			

储	chǔ: store up 储蓄	rén 人(亻) person	储	储	储
	儲 储				
亻 仜	佳 佬	储			

蓄	xù: save up 儲蓄	cǎo 艸(艹) grass	蓄	蓄	蓄
	蓄 蓄				
艹 苎	芸 芸	蓄			

Name: ____________________ Date: ______________

蓄	xù: save up 储蓄	cǎo 艸(艹) grass	蓄	蓄	蓄
	蓄 蓄				
艹 艹 蓄 蓄					

之	zhī: (a particle) 百分之一	piě 丿 left slanted stroke	之	之	之
	之 之				
丶 ㇇ 之					

之	zhī: (a particle) 百分之一	zhǔ 丶 segmentation symbol	之	之	之
	之 之				
丶 ㇇ 之					

支	zhī: pay out or withdraw (支票: cheque) 支票	zhī 支 branch	支	支	支
	支 支				
十 支 支					

職	zhí: duty (職員 : staff) 職員	ěr 耳 ear	職	職	職
	職 職				
𠃍 冂 ⺙ 耳...					

職 (stroke order: 1–18)

zhí: duty (職員 : staff)
職員

ěr 耳
ear

職 职

𠃍	冂	耳	耳	聕	職	職	職

职 (stroke order: 1–11)

zhí: duty (职员 : staff)
职员

ěr 耳
ear

职 职 职

職 职

冂	月	耳	职	职

低 (stroke order: 1–7)

dī: low
利率比較(较)低

rén 人(亻)
person

低 低 低

低 低

亻	亻	亻	亻	低	低

夠 (stroke order: 1–11)

gòu: sufficient
夠了

xī 夕
night

夠 夠 夠

夠 够

夕	夕	多	多	夠	夠

Name: ____________ Date: ____________

够	gòu: sufficient 够了	bāo 勹 wrap	够	够	够
	夠 够				
勹 句	句夕 够				

單	dān: single; bill 單子	kǒu 口 mouth	單	單	單
	單 单				
口 吅	吅日 吅旦 單				

单	dān: single; bill 单子	bā 八 eight	单	单	单
	單 单				
丷 㐄	㐄一 单				

填	tián: fill in 填表	tǔ 土 earth	填	填	填
	填 填				
土 圹	埗 埴 埴 填 填				

千	qiān: thousand 三千元	shí 十 ten	千	千	千
	千 千				
丿 二 千					

元	yuán: dollar 三千元	ér 儿 walking man	元	元	元
	元 元				
一 二 テ 元					

金	jīn: gold 美金	jīn 金 metal	金	金	金
	金 金				
人 亼 全 余 金					

寄	jì: mail, send 寄信	mián 宀 roof	寄	寄	寄
	寄 寄				
宀 宎 宎 奇 寄					

Name: ____________ Date: ____________

簿

bù: book
支票簿

zhú 竹 (⺮)
bamboo

卡

kǎ: card
取款卡

bǔ 卜
predict

當

dāng: (當然: of course)
當然

tián 田
land

当

dāng: (当然: of course)
当然

xiǎo 小
small

換	huàn: exchange 美金換人民幣的匯率	shǒu 手 (扌) hand	換	換	換

換 换

换	huàn: exchange 美金换人民币的汇率	shǒu 手 (扌) hand	换	换	换

換 换

匯	huì: collection (匯率: exchange rate) 匯率	fāng 匚 square vessel	匯	匯	匯

匯 汇

汇	huì: collection 汇率	shuǐ 水 (氵) water	汇	汇	汇

匯 汇

氵 汇

Name: ____________________ Date: ______________

兌	duì: exchange (兑换(換): exchange) 兌換(换)	ér 儿 walking man	兑	兑	兑
	兌 兑				
丷 口	户 兑				

櫃	guì: cabinet 櫃台	mù 木 wood	櫃	櫃	櫃
	櫃 柜				
木 𣏟	𣏟 𣏟	櫃 櫃	櫃 櫃		

柜	guì: cabinet 柜台	mù 木 wood	柜	柜	柜
	櫃 柜				
木 朩	朽 朽	柜			

Name: ____________ Date: ____________

Lesson 7 I Can't Find My Phone Book
第七課 我的電話簿找不到了 (第七课 我的电话簿找不到了)

寒	hán: cold 寒假	mián 宀 roof	寒	寒	寒
	寒 寒				
宀 宀 宀 宀 宀 宀 寒					

遊	yóu: wonder about 旅遊	chuò 辵(辶) motion	遊	遊	遊
	遊 游				
方 方 方 方 方 斿 遊					

游	yóu: wonder about 旅游	shuǐ 水(氵) water	游	游	游
	遊 游				
氵 氵 氵 氵 游					

社	shè: agency, society 旅行社	shì 示 (礻) reveal	社	社	社
	社	社			
礻	礻	礻	社		

訂	dìng: book, order 訂票	yán 言 word	訂	訂	訂
	訂	订			
言	訁一	訂			

订	dìng: book, order 订票	yán 言 (讠) word	订	订	订
	訂	订			
讠	订				

羡	xiàn: admire, envy 羡慕	yáng 羊 sheep	羡	羡	羡
	羡	羡			
丷	䒑	羊	羊氵	羊次	羡

Name: ____________ Date: ____________

羨	xiàn: admire, envy 羨慕		yáng 羊 sheep		羨	羨	羨		
	羨	羡							
丷	䒑	羊	羊	羊	羊	羨			

慕	mù: admire, yearn for 羨慕		xīn 心 (⺗) heart		慕	慕	慕		
	慕	慕							
艹	苜	莫	莫	慕	慕	慕			

慕	mù: admire, yearn for 羨慕		xīn 心 (⺗) heart		慕	慕	慕		
	慕	慕							
艹	苜	莫	莫	慕	慕	慕			

親	qīn: relative (親戚: relative) 親戚		jiàn 見 see		親	親	親		
	親	亲							
亠	立	立	辛	亲	新	親	親		

亲	qīn: relative (亲戚: relative) 亲戚	lì 立 stand	亲	亲	亲
	親 亲				
亠 亣	立 立	辛 亲			

戚	qī: relative (親(亲)戚: relative) 親(亲)戚	gē 戈 spear	戚	戚	戚
	戚 戚				
厂 厈	厈 戚	戚 戚	戚		

原	yuán: primary, original 原來(来)	hàn 厂 shelter	原	原	原
	原 原				
厂 厂	戶 原	原 原			

抽	chōu: extract (抽空: manage to find time) 抽空	shǒu 手 (扌) hand	抽	抽	抽
	抽 抽				
扌 扣	扣 抽	抽			

Name: ________________ Date: ____________

拜	bài: make a courtesy call (拜訪(访): pay a visit) 拜訪(访)	shǒu 手(扌) hand	拜	拜	拜
	拜 拜				
𠂉 手 扌 𢪙 拜					

訪	fǎng: visit (拜訪: pay a visit) 拜訪	yán 言 word	訪	訪	訪
	訪 访				
言 言 訪 訪					

访	fǎng: visit (拜访: pay a visit) 拜访	yán 言(讠) word	访	访	访
	訪 访				
讠 访 访 访					

查	chá: check; investigate; consult 查票	mù 木 wood	查	查	查
	查 查				
十 木 杳 查					

宜	yí: suitable 便宜	mián 宀 roof	宜	宜	宜
	宜 宜				

季	jì: season 四季	zǐ 子 child	季	季	季
	季 季				

季	jì: season 四季	hé 禾 grain	季	季	季
	季 季				

數	shù: number 少數民族	pū 攴(攵) literacy	數	數	數
	數 数				

Name: ____________ Date: ____________

数

shù: number
少数民族

pū 攴(攵)
literacy

数 数 数

數 数

丷 半 米 娄 数 数 数

族

zú: nationality
少數(数)民族

fāng 方
square

族 族 族

族 族

亠 方 方 斿 旌 族

果

guǒ: fruit; result
(如果: if)
如果

mù 木
wood

果 果 果

果 果

冂 曰 旦 甲 果 果

簽

qiān: sign, label
(簽證: visa)
簽證

zhú 竹(⺮)
bamboo

簽 簽 簽

簽 签

⺮ 竺 笒 签 簽 簽

签	qiān: sign, label (签证: visa) 签证	zhú 竹(⺮) bamboo	签	签	签
	簽 签				
⺮ 笶 笅 笭 签					

證	zhèng: certificate (簽證: visa) 簽證	yán 言 word	證	證	證
	證 证				
言 訁 訂 訃 訟 詅 諮 證					

证	zhèng: certificate (签证: visa) 签证	yán 言(讠) word	证	证	证
	證 证				
讠 讠一 订 讦 证 证					

辦	bàn: handle 辦簽證	xīn 辛 pungent	辦	辦	辦
	辦 办				
亠 立 辛 辨 辦 辦 辦					

Name: ____________ Date: ____________

办	bàn: handle 办签证	lì 力 strength	办	办	办
	辦 办				
𠃍 力	办 办				

概	gài: general 大概	mù 木 wood	概	概	概
	概 概				
木 木	相 根	概 概			

及	jí: reach, attain 來得及	yòu 又 right hand	及	及	及
	及 及				
ノ 乃	乃 及				

及	jí: reach, attain 来得及	piě ノ left slanted stroke	及	及	及
	及 及				
ノ 乃	及				

Name: ____________ Date: ____________

Lesson 8 You Are Much Busier Than Before
第八課 你比以前忙得多 (第八课 你比以前忙得多)

連	lián: even 連影子都看不見	chuò 辵(辶) motion	連	連	連
	連 连				
㇐ 亘	車	䢻	連		

连	lián: even 连影子都看不见	chuò 辵(辶) motion	连	连	连
	連 连				
车	车	连			

報	bào: announce 報告	tǔ 土 earth	報	報	報
	報 报				
土	𡈼	幸	報		

报	bào: announce 报告	shǒu 手(扌) hand	报	报	报
	報 报				
扌 扌 扌 扌 报					

告	gào: notify, announce 報(报)告	kǒu 口 mouth	告	告	告
	告 告				
𠂉 牛 生 告					

鬆	sōng: loose, slack 輕鬆	biāo 髟 (of hair) dropping	鬆	鬆	鬆
	鬆 松				
厂 镸 長 髟 髟 髟 鬆					

松	sōng: loose, slack 轻松	mù 木 wood	松	松	松
	鬆 松				
木 木 松 松 松					

Name: ____________ Date: ____________

強	qiáng: strong; better 比我強多了	gōng 弓 bow	強	強	強
	強 強				
㇆ ㇆ 弓 弓 弘 弛 弶 強 強					

强	qiáng: strong; better 比我强多了	gōng 弓 bow	强	强	强
	強 强				
㇆ 弓 弓 弔 弶 强 强					

完	wán: finish, complete 寫(写)完	mián 宀 roof	完	完	完
	完 完				
宀 宀 完 完					

導	dǎo: lead, guide 導演	cùn 寸 inch	導	導	導
	導 导				
丷 丷 首 首 道 道 道 導 導					

导

dǎo: lead, guide
导演

cùn 寸
inch

导 导 导

導 导

コ 巳 导

夫

fū: (功夫: Kong Fu)
功夫片

dà 大
big

夫 夫 夫

夫 夫

一 二 夫 夫

它

tā: it
它的場(场)面

mián 宀
roof

它 它 它

它 它

宀 宀 它

節

jié: part; festival
情節

zhú 竹 (⺮)
bamboo

節 節 節

節 节

⺮ 竻 笴 筤 節 節 節

Name: ________________ Date: ____________

节	jié: part; festival 情节	cǎo 艸(艹) grass	节	节	节
	節 节				
艹 艹 节					

引	yǐn: lead; attract 吸引	gōng 弓 bow	引	引	引
	引 引				
㇆ ㇆ 弓 引					

古	gǔ: ancient 古代	kǒu 口 mouth	古	古	古
	古 古				
一 十 古					

代	dài: historical period; generation 古代	rén 人(亻) person	代	代	代
	代 代				
亻 亻 代 代					

故	gù: reason; old 故事	pū 攴(攵) literacy	故	故	故
	故 故				
十 古 古 古 古 故					

彩	cǎi: color; variety 精彩	shān 彡 fur	彩	彩	彩
	彩 彩				
爫 爫 采 采 彩 彩					

描	miáo: copy; retouch 描寫	shǒu 手(扌) hand	描	描	描
	描 描				
扌 扩 描					

描	miáo: copy; retouch 描写	shǒu 手(扌) hand	描	描	描
	描 描				
扌 扩 描					

Name: ____________________ Date: ______________

歷	lì: go through 歷史	zhǐ 止 stop	歷	歷	歷
	歷 历				
厂 厂	麻 厤	厤 歷			

历	lì: go through 历史	hàn 厂 shelter	历	历	历
	歷 历				
一 厂	万 历				

史	shǐ: history 歷(历)史	kǒu 口 mouth	史	史	史
	史 史				
口 中	史				

趣	qù: interest 興(兴)趣	zǒu 走 walk	趣	趣	趣
	趣 趣				
土 丰	走 赱	趄 趐	趣 趣		

而

ér: (而且: also, in addition) 而且

ér 而 and

而 而 而

而 而

丆 丆 丙 丙 而

且

qiě: (而且: also, in addition) 而且

yī 一 one

且 且 且

且 且

冂 月 目 且

技

jì: skill 特技

shǒu 手 (扌) hand

技 技 技

技 技

扌 扌 技

效

xiào: effect 效果

pū 攴(攵) literacy

效 效 效

效 效

亠 六 交 效 效 效

Name: ______________ Date: ______________

顏	yán: color 顏色	yè 頁 head	顏	顏	顏
	顏 颜				
亠 文	产 彦 彦	顏 顏 顏			

颜	yán: color 颜色	yè 頁 (页) head	颜	颜	颜
	顏 颜				
立 产	彦 彦 彦	颜 颜			

週	zhōu: week; circuit 週末	chuò 辵(辶) motion	週	週	週
	週 周				
丿 冂	円 周 调	週			

周	zhōu: week; circuit 周末	jiōng 冂 borders	周	周	周
	週 周				
丿 冂	円 周				

末

mò: end
週(周)末

mù 木
wood

末 末 末

末 末

〓 丰 耒 末

價

jià: price, value
票價

rén 人(亻)
person

價 價 價

價 价

亻 亻 价 價 價 價 價 價

价

jià: price, value
票价

rén 人(亻)
person

价 价 价

價 价

亻 价 价 价

Name: ________________ Date: ____________

Lesson 9 You Are Getting More and More Energetic
第九課 你越來越精神了 (第九课 你越来越精神了)

越	yuè: exceed 越來(来)越精神了	zǒu 走 walk	越	越	越
	越 越				
走	走	赱	赾	越	越

需	xū: need 需要	yǔ 雨 rain	需	需	需
	需 需				
二	雨	雨	雨	雨	需	需

瘦	shòu: thin 瘦了不少	nè 疒 sick	瘦	瘦	瘦
	瘦 瘦				
亠	广	疒	疒	疒	疒	瘦	瘦

瘦	shòu: thin 瘦了不少	nè 疒 sick	瘦	瘦	瘦
	瘦 瘦				
疒	疒	疒	疒	疒	疒	疒	瘦

減	jiǎn: reduce 減肥	shuǐ 水(氵) water	減	減	減
	減 減				
氵	氵	氵	氵	減	減

减	jiǎn: reduce 减肥	bīng 冫 ice	减	减	减
	减 减				
冫	冫	冫	冫	冫	减	减	减

肥	féi: fat 減(减)肥	ròu 肉 (月) meat	肥	肥	肥
	肥 肥				
月	月	月	肥

Name: ________________ Date: ____________

堅	jiān: hard, firm 堅持	tǔ 土 earth	堅	堅	堅
	堅 坚				

堅 坚

坚	jiān: hard, firm 坚持	tǔ 土 earth	坚	坚	坚
	堅 坚				

坚

持	chí: keep, maintain 堅(坚)持	shǒu 手 (扌) hand	持	持	持
	持 持				

扌 扗 持

磅	bàng: pound 二十幾(几)磅	shí 石 stone	磅	磅	磅
	磅 磅				

石 磅

怪	guài: strange 怪不得	xīn 心 (忄) heart	怪	怪	怪
	怪 怪				
忄 怊 怪					

苗	miáo: (苗條: slim) 苗條	cǎo 艸 (艹) grass	苗	苗	苗
	苗 苗				
艹 苗					

苗	miáo: (苗条: slim) 苗条	cǎo 艸 (艹) grass	苗	苗	苗
	苗 苗				
艹 苗					

孩	hái: child 女孩子	zǐ 子 child	孩	孩	孩
	孩 孩				
乛 子 孑 孒 孩 孩					

Name: ____________________ Date: ________________

控	kòng: control 控制	shǒu 手 (扌) hand	控	控	控
	控	控			

Stroke sequence: 扌 扩 护 控

制	zhì: control 控制	dāo 刀 (刂) knife	制	制	制
	制	制			

Stroke sequence: 𠂉 ⺈ 肀 朱 制

飲	yǐn: drink 飲食	shí 食 (飠) food	飲	飲	飲
	飲	饮			

Stroke sequence: 𠆢 今 今 食 食 飠 飲 飲

饮	yǐn: drink 饮食	shí 食 (饣) food	饮	饮	饮
	飲	饮			

Stroke sequence: 𠂊 饣 饮 饮

食	shí: food 飲(饮)食	shí 食 (飠) food	食	食	食

食 食

Stroke order: 人 今 今 今 飠 食

注	zhù: concentrate 注意	shuǐ 水 (氵) water	注	注	注

注 注

Stroke order: 氵 汁 汼 泩 注

甜	tián: sweet 甜食	gān 甘 sweet	甜	甜	甜

甜 甜

Stroke order: 二 舌 舌一 舌卜 甜 甜 甜

甜	tián: sweet 甜食	shé 舌 tongue	甜	甜	甜

甜 甜

Stroke order: 丿 二 千 舌 舌卜 甜 甜 甜

Name: ________________ Date: ____________

早	zǎo: early 早就想	rì 日 sun	早	早	早
	早 早				
日 旦 早					

矮	ǎi: (of stature) short 個(个)子矮	shǐ 矢 arrow	矮	矮	矮
	矮 矮				
𠂉 𠂉 矢 矢 矢 矮 矮					

呎	chǐ: (a unit of length) foot 五呎一吋	kǒu 口 mouth	呎	呎	呎
	呎 呎				
口 口 口 吚 呎					

吋	cùn: (a unit of length) inch 五呎一吋	kǒu 口 mouth	吋	吋	吋
	吋 吋				
口 口一 吋 吋					

超	chāo: exceed 超過(过)	zǒu 走 walk	超	超	超
	超 超				
土 丰	走 起 起 超				

靈	líng: quick, clever 靈活	yǔ 雨 rain	靈	靈	靈
	靈 灵				
冖	靈				

灵	líng: quick, clever 灵活	huǒ 火 fire	灵	灵	灵
	靈 灵				
	灵				

總	all, general 總是	mì 糸(纟) silk	總	總	總
	總 总				
幺 糸	總				

Name: ________________ Date: ____________

总	all, general 总是	xīn 心(忄) heart	总	总	总
	總 总				
丷	总	总			

更	gèng: even, more 比以前更瘦	yuē 曰 say	更	更	更
	更 更				
一	百	更	更		

更	gèng: even, more 比以前更瘦	yī 一 one	更	更	更
	更 更				
一	百	更	更		

Name: ____________ Date: ____________

Lesson 10 My Plan for the Winter Vacation – Review
第十課 我的寒假計畫–復習 (第十课 我的寒假计划–复习)

希

xī: hope
希望(望)

jīn 巾
napkin

希 希 希 希 希

丿 乂 㐅 产 肴 希

望

wàng: hope
希望(望)

ròu 肉 (月)
meat

望 望 望 望 望

亠 亡 访 访 望 望 望

旬

xún: a period of ten days
上旬

rì 日
sun

旬 旬 旬 旬 旬

丿 勹 旬

受	shòu: receive 接受	yòu 又 right hand	受	受	受
	受 受				
丿 爫	爫 孚 受				

商	shāng: trade, business 商店	kǒu 口 mouth	商	商	商
	商 商				
亠 ⺈	产 产 商				

根	gēn: root, base 根據(据)	mù 木 wood	根	根	根
	根 根				
木 木ヨ	相 相 根				

據	jù: depend on 根據	shǒu 手(扌) hand	據	據	據
	據 据				
扌 扌⺊	扩 扩 护 捞 據 據				

Name: ________________ Date: ____________

据	jù: depend on 根据	shǒu 手 (扌) hand	据	据	据
	據 据				
扌	扌	护	护	据	

零	líng: zero 零點(点)一	yǔ 雨 rain	零	零	零
	零 零				

爬	pá: climb 爬長(长)城	zhǎo 爪 (爫) claw	爬	爬	爬
	爬 爬				

頂	dǐng: summit 山頂	yè 頁 head	頂	頂	頂
	頂 顶				

顶	dǐng: summit 山顶	yè 頁 (页) head	顶	顶	顶
	頂	顶			
丁	丁	丁	顶	顶	顶

助	zhù: aid, help 幫(帮)助	lì 力 strength	助	助	助
	助	助			
冂	月	且	助	助	

漢	hàn: man 好漢	shuǐ 水 (氵) water	漢	漢	漢
	漢	汉			
氵	泄	泄	浩	漟	漢	漢

汉	hàn: man 好汉	shuǐ 水 (氵) water	汉	汉	汉
	漢	汉			
氵	汉				

Name: ____________ Date: ____________

訴	sù: tell 告訴	yán 言 word	訴	訴	訴
	訴	诉			
言	訁	訢	訢	訴	

诉	sù: tell 告诉	yán 言 word	诉	诉	诉
	訴	诉			
讠	讠	讠	诉	诉	

壯	zhuàng: strong; grand 壯觀	qiáng 爿 slit wood	壯	壯	壯
	壯	壮			
丬	丬	爿	壯	壯	

壮	zhuàng: strong; grand 壮观	shì 士 person	壮	壮	壮
	壯	壮			
丶	冫	丬	壮		

曲

qū: bend, crooked
曲折

yuē 曰
say

曲 曲 曲

曲 曲

冂 冃 冄 冊 曲

折

zhé: bend, twist
曲折

shǒu 手 (扌)
hand

折 折 折

折 折

扌 扩 扩 折

載

zài: to carry,
be loaded with
滿載而歸

chē 車
vehicle

載 載 載

載 载

土 吉 車 載 載 載

载

zài: to carry,
be loaded with
满载而归

chē 車 (车)
vehicle

载 载 载

載 载

土 査 査 载 载 载

Name: ____________________ Date: ______________

歸	guī: return 滿載而歸	zhǐ 止 stop	歸	歸	歸
	歸	归			
丿	𠂆	𠂤			歸

归	guī: return 满载而归	jì 彐 snout	归	归	归
	歸	归			
丨	刂	归			

寫字簿生字索引-繁體字 CHARACTER BOOK INDEX – TRADITIONAL CHARACTER VERSION (BY NUMBER OF STROKES)

Each entry lists traditional character, simplified character, Pinyin, English meaning, and lesson number:

2

刀	刀	dāo	knife	2

3

己	己	jǐ	oneself	2
叉	叉	chā	cross	3
口	口	kǒu	mouth, entrance	3
山	山	shān	mountain	3
之	之	zhī	(a particle)	6
千	千	qiān	thousand	6

4

片	片	piàn	thin piece	2
化	化	huà	變化: change	3
尺	尺	chǐ	ruler	3
戶	户	hù	door; (bank) account	6
支	支	zhī	to pay out; withdraw	6
元	元	yuán	dollar	6
及	及	jí	to reach, attain	7
夫	夫	fū	功夫: Kung Fu	8
引	引	yǐn	to lead, attract	8

5

主	主	zhǔ	主意: idea	1
北	北	běi	north	2
台	台	tái	stage, platform	2
左	左	zuǒ	left	3
田	田	tián	field	3
右	右	yòu	right	3
民	民	mín	people	3
母	母	mǔ	mother	4
永	永	yǒng	forever	4
乎	乎	hū	(a particle expressing doubt or conjecture)	4
卡	卡	kǎ	card	6
它	它	tā	it	8
古	古	gǔ	ancient	8
代	代	dài	historical period; generation	8
史	史	shǐ	history	8
且	且	qiě	而且: also, in addition	8
末	末	mò	end	8

6

合	合	hé	to combine	1
衣	衣	yī	clothes	1
死	死	sǐ	dead	1
各	各	gè	each, every	2
全	全	quán	whole; intact	3
交	交	jiāo	(of places or periods of time) meet, join	3
成	成	chéng	to become	3
向	向	xiàng	to, towards	3
亦	亦	yì	also	4
存	存	cún	to deposit	6
而	而	ér	而且: also, in addition	8
早	早	zǎo	early	9
吋	吋	cùn	inch	9
旬	旬	xún	a period of ten days	10
曲	曲	qū	bend, crooked	10

站	站	zhàn	to stand	2
乘	乘	chéng	to take (a ship, plane, etc.)	3
航	航	háng	to navigate	3
展	展	zhǎn	to stretch	3
素	素	sù	basic element	4
特	特	tè	specially	4
差	差	chāi	errand, job	4
俱	俱	jù	all, completely	4
笑	笑	xiào	to laugh	5
值	值	zhí	to be worth	5
原	原	yuán	primary, original	7
連	连	lián	even	8
效	效	xiào	effect	8
根	根	gēn	root, base	10

11

責	责	zé	duty	1
掃	扫	sǎo	to sweep	1
理	理	lǐ	to put in order	1
掛	挂	guà	to hang	1
累	累	lèi	tired	1
衆	众	zhòng	multitude	2
康	康	kāng	healthy	4
涼	凉	liáng	cool, cold	4
眼	眼	yǎn	eye	4
乾	干	gān	dry; to empty	4
陰	阴	yīn	overcast	5
終	终	zhōng	end	5
情	情	qíng	affection	5
帳	账	zhàng	account	6
率	率	lǜ	rate	6
夠	够	gòu	sufficient	6
寄	寄	jì	to mail, send	6
戚	戚	qī	relative	7
訪	访	fǎng	to visit	7
族	族	zú	nationality	7
強	强	qiáng	strong; better	8
彩	彩	cǎi	color; variety	8
週	周	zhōu	week; circuit	8
堅	坚	jiān	hard, firm	9
控	控	kòng	to control	9
甜	甜	tián	sweet	9
望	望	wàng	to hope	10
商	商	shāng	trade, business	10
頂	顶	dǐng	summit	10

12

窗	窗	chuāng	window	1
著	着	zhe	(a particle indicating an aspect)	2
琴	琴	qín	a general name mostly for string instruments	2
畫	画	huà	to draw, paint	2
棟	栋	dòng	(measure word for buildings)	3
喔	喔	ō	(an interjection indicating sudden realization)	3
費	费	fèi	cost, expenditure	3
睏	困	kùn	sleepy	4
街	街	jiē	street	4
款	款	kuǎn	a sum of money	6
單	单	dān	single; bill	6
換	换	huàn	to exchange	6
寒	寒	hán	cold	7
遊	游	yóu	to wander about	7
報	报	bào	to announce	8
描	描	miáo	to copy, retouch	8
越	越	yuè	to exceed	9
減	减	jiǎn	to reduce	9
飲	饮	yǐn	drink	9
超	超	chāo	to exceed	9
訴	诉	sù	to tell	10

13

裝	装	zhuāng	to install; clothes	1
照	照	zhào	to take (pictures)	2
鼓	鼓	gǔ	drum	2
落	落	luò	to drop, land	3
搭	搭	dā	to take (a ship, plane, etc.)	3
農	农	nóng	agriculture	3
睛	睛	jīng	eyeball	4
飽	饱	bǎo	to be full	4
廈	厦	shà	tall building	5

填	填	tián	to fill in	6
當	当	dāng	當然: of course	6
匯	汇	huì	collection	6
羨	羡	xiàn	to admire, envy	7
概	概	gài	general	7
節	节	jié	part; festival	8
矮	矮	ǎi	short	9
零	零	líng	zero	10
載	载	zài	to carry, be loaded with	10

14

種	种	zhǒng	kind, type	2
演	演	yǎn	to perform, play	2
滿	满	mǎn	full	2
算	算	suàn	to plan, calculate	3
幣	币	bì	money, currency	3
維	维	wéi	to maintain	4
輕	轻	qīng	small in degree	4
精	精	jīng	energy, spirit	4
適	适	shì	fit, suitable	4
慣	惯	guàn	to be in the habit of	4
聚	聚	jù	to gather	4
誤	误	wù	to miss	5
趕	赶	gǎn	to catch, take	5
團	团	tuán	group	5
榮	荣	róng	glory	5
銀	银	yín	silver	6
蓄	蓄	xù	to save up	6
需	需	xū	need	9
漢	汉	hàn	man	10

15

撞	撞	zhuàng	to collide	1
箱	箱	xiāng	box, case	1
彈	弹	tán	to play (a musical instrument), pluck	2
髮	发	fà	hair	4
鬧	闹	nào	to do, make	5
慕	慕	mù	to admire, yarn for	7
數	数	shù	number	7
導	导	dǎo	to lead, guide	8
趣	趣	qù	interest	8
價	价	jià	price, value	8
瘦	瘦	shòu	thin	9
磅	磅	bàng	pound	9

16

樹	树	shù	tree	1
整	整	zhěng	to put in order	1
器	器	qì	utensil, ware	2
燈	灯	dēng	light, lamp	3
親	亲	qīn	relative	7
辦	办	bàn	to handle	7
歷	历	lì	to go through	8
據	据	jù	to depend on	10

17

牆	墙	qiáng	wall	2
戲	戏	xì	traditional Chinese opera	2
臉	脸	liǎn	face	2
繁	繁	fán	numerous, grand	5
雖	虽	suī	although	5
儲	储	chǔ	to store up	6
職	职	zhí	duty	6
總	总	zǒng	all, general	9

18

擺	摆	bǎi	to put, place	2
轉	转	zhuǎn	to turn	3
櫃	柜	guì	cabinet	6
鬆	松	sōng	loose, slack	8
顏	颜	yán	color	8
歸	归	guī	to return	10

19

壞	坏	huài	bad	1
鏡	镜	jìng	mirror	1
繫	系	jì	to fasten	3
簿	簿	bù	book	6
簽	签	qiān	to sign, label	7
證	证	zhèng	certificate	7

写字簿生字索引–简体字　CHARACTER BOOK INDEX – SIMPLIFIED CHARACTER VERSION (BY NUMBER OF STROKES)

Each entry lists simplified character, traditional character, Pinyin, English meaning, and lesson number:

2

刀	刀	dāo	knife	2

3

己	己	jǐ	oneself	2
叉	叉	chā	cross	3
口	口	kǒu	mouth, entrance	3
山	山	shān	mountain	3
干	幹	gān	dry; to empty	4
于	於	yú	终于: at last	5
之	之	zhī	(a particle)	6
千	千	qiān	thousand	6
及	及	jí	to reach, attain	7

4

片	片	piàn	thin piece	2
长	長	cháng	long	2
计	計	jì	to count, calculate	3
化	化	huà	变化: change	3
尺	尺	chǐ	ruler	3
币	幣	bì	money, currency	3
户	戶	hù	door; (bank) account	6
支	支	zhī	to pay out; withdraw	6
元	元	yuán	dollar	6
订	訂	dìng	to book, order	7
办	辦	bàn	to handle	7
连	連	lián	even	8
夫	夫	fū	功夫: Kung Fu	8
引	引	yǐn	to lead, attract	8
历	歷	lì	to go through	8

5

主	主	zhǔ	主意: idea	1
北	北	běi	north	2
出	齣	chū	(measure word for dramas)	2
台	台	tái	stage, platform	2
左	左	zuǒ	left	3
田	田	tián	field	3
右	右	yòu	right	3
民	民	mín	people	3
母	母	mǔ	mother	4
永	永	yǒng	forever	4
乎	乎	hū	(a particle expressing doubt or conjecture)	4
团	團	tuán	group	5
卡	卡	kǎ	card	6
汇	匯	huì	collection	6
它	它	tā	it	8
节	節	jié	part; festival	8
古	古	gǔ	ancient	8
代	代	dài	historical period; generation	8
史	史	shǐ	history	8
且	且	qiě	而且: also, in addition	8
末	末	mò	end	8
汉	漢	hàn	man	10
归	歸	guī	to return	10

6

合	合	hé	to combine	1
负	負	fù	to bear	1
扫	掃	sǎo	to sweep	1

衣	衣	yī	clothes	1
死	死	sǐ	dead	1
各	各	gè	each, every	2
戏	戲	xì	traditional Chinese opera	2
众	眾	zhòng	multitude	2
全	全	quán	whole; intact	3
交	交	jiāo	(of places or periods of time) meet, join	3
农	農	nóng	agriculture	3
成	成	chéng	to become	3
灯	燈	dēng	light, lamp	3
向	向	xiàng	to, towards	3
亦	亦	yì	also	4
阴	陰	yīn	overcast	5
存	存	cún	to deposit	6
当	當	dāng	当然: of course	6
访	訪	fǎng	to visit	7
导	導	dǎo	to lead, guide	8
而	而	ér	而且: also, in addition	8
价	價	jià	price, value	8
早	早	zǎo	early	9
吋	吋	cùn	inch	9
旬	旬	xún	a period of ten days	10
壮	壯	zhuàng	strong; grand	10
曲	曲	qū	bend, crooked	10

7

别	別	bié	don't	1
坏	壞	huài	bad	1
呀	呀	ya	(indicating surprise)	1
李	李	lǐ	行李: luggage	1
附	附	fù	be near	1
忘	忘	wàng	to forget	1
系	繫	jì	to fasten	3
里	里	lǐ	公里: kilometer	3
花	花	huā	(of eyes) blurred	4
困	睏	kùn	sleepy	4
利	利	lì	profit, interest	6
低	低	dī	low	6
兑	兌	duì	to exchange	6
社	社	shè	agency, society	7
证	證	zhèng	certificate	7
报	報	bào	to announce	8
告	告	gào	to notify, announce	8
完	完	wán	finish, complete	8
技	技	jì	skill	8
坚	堅	jiān	hard, firm	9
饮	飲	yǐn	drink	9
呎	呎	chǐ	(a unit of length) foot	9
灵	靈	líng	quick, clever	9
更	更	gèng	even, more	9
希	希	xī	to hope	10
助	助	zhù	to aid, help	10
诉	訴	sù	to tell	10
折	折	zhé	to bend, twist	10

8

责	責	zé	duty	1
表	表	biǎo	表演: to perform, play	2
拉	拉	lā	to play (certain musical instruments)	2
画	畫	huà	to draw, paint	2
往	往	wǎng	to, towards	3
降	降	jiàng	to fall, lower	3
拐	拐	guǎi	to turn	3
直	直	zhí	straight	3
变	變	biàn	to change	3
转	轉	zhuǎn	to turn	3
发	髮	fà	hair	4
味	味	wèi	taste	4
饱	飽	bǎo	to be full	4
终	終	zhōng	end	5
闹	鬧	nào	to do, make	5
账	帳	zhàng	account	6
取	取	qǔ	to take, withdraw	6
单	單	dān	single; bill	6
金	金	jīn	gold	6
柜	櫃	guì	cabinet	6
抽	抽	chōu	to extract	7
宜	宜	yí	suitable	7
季	季	jì	season	7
果	果	guǒ	fruit; result	7
松	鬆	sōng	loose, slack	8

周	週	zhōu	week; circuit	8
肥	肥	féi	fat	9
怪	怪	guài	strange	9
苗	苗	miáo	苗条: slim	9
制	制	zhì	to control	9
注	注	zhù	to concentrate	9
受	受	shòu	to receive	10
爬	爬	pá	to climb	10
顶	頂	dǐng	summit	10

9

树	樹	shù	tree	1
挂	掛	guà	to hang	1
咱	咱	zán	we (including both the speaker and the person/s spoken to)	1
种	種	zhǒng	kind, type	2
胡	胡	hú	barbarian, (胡琴: two-string bow instrument)	2
奏	奏	zòu	to play (a musical instrument), pluck	2
神	神	shén	spirit	2
品	品	pǐn	article, product	3
栋	棟	dòng	(measure word for buildings)	3
弯	彎	wān	curve	3
费	費	fèi	cost, expenditure	3
轻	輕	qīng	small in degree	4
适	適	shì	fit, suitable	4
香	香	xiāng	aroma, good smell	4
便	便	biàn	convenient	4
相	相	xiāng	mutually	4
误	誤	wù	to miss	5
津	津	jīn	saliva	5
界	界	jiè	boundary	5
荣	榮	róng	glory	5
虽	雖	suī	although	5
挺	挺	tǐng	very, quite	5
亲	親	qīn	relative	7
拜	拜	bài	to make a courtesy call	7
查	查	chá	to check, investigate, consult	7
故	故	gù	reason, old	8
持	持	chí	to keep, maintain	9
孩	孩	hái	child	9
食	食	shí	food	9
总	總	zǒng	all, general	9

10

倒	倒	dào	to move backward	1
破	破	pò	broken	1
套	套	tào	cover	1
拿	拿	ná	to hold	2
座	座	zuò	seat	2
站	站	zhàn	to stand	2
乘	乘	chéng	to take (a ship, plane, etc.)	3
航	航	háng	to navigate	3
展	展	zhǎn	to stretch	3
素	素	sù	basic element	4
特	特	tè	specially	4
凉	涼	liáng	cool, cold	4
差	差	chāi	errand, job	4
俱	俱	jù	all, completely	4
赶	趕	gǎn	to catch, take	5
笑	笑	xiào	to laugh	5
值	值	zhí	to be worth	5
换	換	huàn	to exchange	6
原	原	yuán	primary, original	7
效	效	xiào	effect	8
根	根	gēn	root, base	10
载	載	zài	to carry, be loaded with	10

11

理	理	lǐ	to put in order	1
累	累	lèi	tired	1
着	著	zhe	(a particle indicating an aspect)	2
弹	彈	tán	to play (a musical instrument), pluck	2
脸	臉	liǎn	face	2
维	維	wéi	to maintain	4
康	康	kāng	healthy	4
眼	眼	yǎn	eye	4
惯	慣	guàn	to be in the habit of	4

寫字簿生字索引–課文 CHARACTER BOOK INDEX (BY LESSON NUMBER)

Each entry lists traditional character, simplified character, Pinyin, and English meaning:

Lesson 1

倒	倒	dào	to move backward
別	别	bié	don't
樹	树	shù	tree
撞	撞	zhuàng	to collide
壞	坏	huài	bad
呀	呀	ya	(indicating surprise)
鏡	镜	jìng	mirror
破	破	pò	broken
合	合	hé	to combine
主	主	zhǔ	主意: idea
負	负	fù	to bear
責	责	zé	duty
李	李	lǐ	行李: luggage
裝	装	zhuāng	to install; clothes
掃	扫	sǎo	to sweep
整	整	zhěng	to put in order
理	理	lǐ	to put in order
箱	箱	xiāng	box, case
衣	衣	yī	clothes
掛	挂	guà	to hang
累	累	lèi	tired
死	死	sǐ	dead
附	附	fù	be near
忘	忘	wàng	to forget
窗	窗	chuāng	window
套	套	tào	cover
咱	咱	zán	we (including both the speaker and the person/s spoken to)

Lesson 2

牆	墙	qiáng	wall
著	着	zhe	(a particle indicating an aspect)
照	照	zhào	to take (pictures)
片	片	piàn	thin piece
北	北	běi	north
台	台	tái	stage, platform
擺	摆	bǎi	to put, place
各	各	gè	each, every
種	种	zhǒng	kind, type
器	器	qì	utensil, ware
演	演	yǎn	to perform, play
表	表	biǎo	表演: to perform, play
鼓	鼓	gǔ	drum
拉	拉	lā	to play (certain musical instruments)
胡	胡	hú	barbarian, (胡琴: two-string bow instrument)
琴	琴	qín	a general name mostly for string instruments
彈	弹	tán	to play (a musical instrument), pluck
奏	奏	zòu	to play (a musical instrument)
己	己	jǐ	oneself
齣	出	chū	(measure word for dramas)
戲	戏	xì	traditional Chinese opera
畫	画	huà	to draw, paint
臉	脸	liǎn	face
拿	拿	ná	to hold
刀	刀	dāo	knife
神	神	shén	spirit
座	座	zuò	seat
滿	满	mǎn	full
眾	众	zhòng	multitude
站	站	zhàn	to stand
長	长	cháng	long

Lesson 3

往	往	wǎng	to, towards
降	降	jiàng	to fall, lower
落	落	luò	to drop, land
全	全	quán	whole; intact
繫	系	jì	to fasten
計	计	jì	to count, calculate
算	算	suàn	to plan, calculate
品	品	pǐn	article, product
搭	搭	dā	to take (a ship, plane, etc.)
乘	乘	chéng	to take (a ship, plane, etc.)
航	航	háng	to navigate
棟	栋	dòng	(measure word for buildings)
交	交	jiāo	(of places or periods of time) meet, join
叉	叉	chā	cross
口	口	kǒu	mouth, entrance
左	左	zuǒ	left
拐	拐	guǎi	to turn
直	直	zhí	straight
里	里	lǐ	公里: kilometer
展	展	zhǎn	to stretch
變	变	biàn	to change
化	化	huà	變化: change
農	农	nóng	agriculture
田	田	tián	field
成	成	chéng	to become
喔	喔	ō	(an interjection indicating sudden realization)
尺	尺	chǐ	ruler
山	山	shān	mountain
燈	灯	dēng	light, lamp
向	向	xiàng	to, towards
右	右	yòu	right
轉	转	zhuǎn	to turn
彎	弯	wān	curve
費	费	fèi	cost, expenditure
民	民	mín	people
幣	币	bì	money, currency

Lesson 4

母	母	mǔ	mother
維	维	wéi	to maintain
素	素	sù	basic element
永	永	yǒng	forever
康	康	kāng	healthy
輕	轻	qīng	small in degree
特	特	tè	specially
涼	凉	liáng	cool, cold
精	精	jīng	energy, spirit
髮	发	fà	hair
眼	眼	yǎn	eye
睛	睛	jīng	eyeball
花	花	huā	(of eyes) blurred
適	适	shì	fit, suitable
差	差	chāi	errand, job
睏	困	kùn	sleepy
街	街	jiē	street
慣	惯	guàn	to be in the habit of
味	味	wèi	taste
香	香	xiāng	aroma, good smell
俱	俱	jù	all, completely
飽	饱	bǎo	to be full
便	便	biàn	convenient
相	相	xiāng	mutually
聚	聚	jù	to gather
乾	干	gān	dry; to empty
亦	亦	yì	also
乎	乎	hū	(a particle expressing doubt or conjecture)

Lesson 5

陰	阴	yīn	overcast
終	终	zhōng	end
於	于	yú	終於: at last
誤	误	wù	to miss
趕	赶	gǎn	to catch, take
情	情	qíng	affection
津	津	jīn	saliva
界	界	jiè	boundary
團	团	tuán	group
鬧	闹	nào	to do, make
笑	笑	xiào	to laugh

繁	繁	fán	numerous, grand
榮	荣	róng	glory
廈	厦	shà	tall building
雖	虽	suī	although
挺	挺	tǐng	very, quite
值	值	zhí	to be worth

Lesson 6

銀	银	yín	silver
帳	账	zhàng	account
戶	户	hù	door; (bank) account
存	存	cún	to deposit
款	款	kuǎn	a sum of money
取	取	qǔ	to take, withdraw
利	利	lì	profit, interest
率	率	lǜ	rate
儲	储	chǔ	to store up
蓄	蓄	xù	to save up
之	之	zhī	(a particle)
支	支	zhī	to pay out; withdraw
職	职	zhí	duty
低	低	dī	low
夠	够	gòu	sufficient
單	单	dān	single; bill
填	填	tián	to fill in
千	千	qiān	thousand
元	元	yuán	dollar
金	金	jīn	gold
寄	寄	jì	to mail, send
簿	簿	bù	book
卡	卡	kǎ	card
當	当	dāng	當然: of course
換	换	huàn	to exchange
匯	汇	huì	collection
兌	兑	duì	to exchange
櫃	柜	guì	cabinet

Lesson 7

寒	寒	hán	cold
遊	游	yóu	to wander about
社	社	shè	agency, society
訂	订	dìng	to book, order
羨	羡	xiàn	to admire, envy
慕	慕	mù	to admire, yarn for
親	亲	qīn	relative
戚	戚	qī	relative
原	原	yuán	primary, original
抽	抽	chōu	to extract
拜	拜	bài	to make a courtesy call
訪	访	fǎng	to visit
查	查	chá	to check, investigate, consult
宜	宜	yí	suitable
季	季	jì	season
數	数	shù	number
族	族	zú	nationality
果	果	guǒ	fruit; result
簽	签	qiān	to sign, label
證	证	zhèng	certificate
辦	办	bàn	to handle
概	概	gài	general
及	及	jí	to reach, attain

Lesson 8

連	连	lián	even
報	报	bào	to announce
告	告	gào	to notify, announce
鬆	松	sōng	loose, slack
強	强	qiáng	strong; better
完	完	wán	finish, complete
導	导	dǎo	to lead, guide
夫	夫	fū	功夫: Kung Fu
它	它	tā	it
節	节	jié	part; festival
引	引	yǐn	to lead, attract
古	古	gǔ	ancient
代	代	dài	historical period; generation
故	故	gù	reason, old
彩	彩	cǎi	color; variety
描	描	miáo	to copy, retouch
歷	历	lì	to go through
史	史	shǐ	history
趣	趣	qù	interest
而	而	ér	而且: also, in addition
且	且	qiě	而且: also, in addition
技	技	jì	skill

效	效	xiào	effect
顏	颜	yán	color
週	周	zhōu	week; circuit
末	末	mò	end
價	价	jià	price, value

Lesson 9

越	越	yuè	to exceed
需	需	xū	need
瘦	瘦	shòu	thin
減	减	jiǎn	to reduce
肥	肥	féi	fat
堅	坚	jiān	hard, firm
持	持	chí	to keep, maintain
磅	磅	bàng	pound
怪	怪	guài	strange
苗	苗	miáo	苗條: slim
孩	孩	hái	child
控	控	kòng	to control
制	制	zhì	to control
飲	饮	yǐn	drink
食	食	shí	food
注	注	zhù	to concentrate
甜	甜	tián	sweet
早	早	zǎo	early
矮	矮	ǎi	short

呎	呎	chǐ	(a unit of length) foot
吋	吋	cùn	inch
超	超	chāo	to exceed
靈	灵	líng	quick, clever
總	总	zǒng	all, general
更	更	gèng	even, more

Lesson 10

希	希	xī	to hope
望	望	wàng	to hope
旬	旬	xún	a period of ten days
受	受	shòu	to receive
商	商	shāng	trade, business
根	根	gēn	root, base
據	据	jù	to depend on
零	零	líng	zero
爬	爬	pá	to climb
頂	顶	dǐng	summit
助	助	zhù	to aid, help
漢	汉	hàn	man
訴	诉	sù	to tell
壯	壮	zhuàng	strong; grand
曲	曲	qū	bend, crooked
折	折	zhé	to bend, twist
載	载	zài	to carry, be loaded with
歸	归	guī	to return

寫字簿生字索引–拼音 CHARACTER BOOK INDEX (ALPHABETICAL BY PINYIN)

Each entry lists traditional character, simplified character, Pinyin, English meaning, and lesson number:

A

矮	矮	ǎi	short	9

B

擺	摆	bǎi	to put, place	2
拜	拜	bài	to make a courtesy call	7
辦	办	bàn	to handle	7
磅	磅	bàng	pound	9
飽	饱	bǎo	to be full	4
報	报	bào	to announce	8
北	北	běi	north	2
幣	币	bì	money, currency	3
變	变	biàn	to change	3
便	便	biàn	convenient	4
表	表	biǎo	表演: to perform, play	2
别	别	bié	don't	1
簿	簿	bù	book	6

C

彩	彩	cǎi	color; variety	8
叉	叉	chā	cross	3
差	差	chāi	errand, job	4
查	查	chá	to check, investigate, consult	7
長	长	cháng	long	2
超	超	chāo	to exceed	9
乘	乘	chéng	to take (a ship, plane, etc.)	3
成	成	chéng	to become	3
持	持	chí	to keep, maintain	9
尺	尺	chǐ	ruler	3
呎	呎	chǐ	(a unit of length) foot	9
抽	抽	chōu	to extract	7
齣	出	chū	(measure word for dramas)	2
儲	储	chǔ	to store up	6
窗	窗	chuāng	window	1
存	存	cún	to deposit	6
吋	吋	cùn	inch	9

D

搭	搭	dā	to take (a ship, plane, etc.)	3
代	代	dài	historical period; generation	8
單	单	dān	single; bill	6
當	当	dāng	當然: of course	6
刀	刀	dāo	knife	2
導	导	dǎo	to lead, guide	8
倒	倒	dào	to move backward	1
燈	灯	dēng	light, lamp	3
低	低	dī	low	6
頂	顶	dǐng	summit	10
訂	订	dìng	to book, order	7
棟	栋	dòng	(measure word for buildings)	3
兑	兑	duì	to exchange	6

E

而	而	ér	而且: also, in addition	8

F

髮	发	fà	hair	4
繁	繁	fán	numerous, grand	5
訪	访	fǎng	to visit	7

肥	肥	féi	fat	9
費	费	fèi	cost, expenditure	3
夫	夫	fū	功夫: Kung Fu	8
負	负	fù	to bear	1
附	附	fù	be near	1

G

概	概	gài	general	7
乾	干	gān	dry; to empty	4
趕	赶	gǎn	to catch, take	5
告	告	gào	to notify, announce	8
各	各	gè	each, every	2
根	根	gēn	root, base	10
更	更	gèng	even, more	9
夠	够	gòu	sufficient	6
古	古	gǔ	ancient	8
鼓	鼓	gǔ	drum	2
故	故	gù	reason, old	8
掛	挂	guà	to hang	1
拐	拐	guǎi	to turn	3
怪	怪	guài	strange	9
慣	惯	guàn	to be in the habit of	4
歸	归	guī	to return	10
櫃	柜	guì	cabinet	6
果	果	guǒ	fruit; result	7

H

孩	孩	hái	child	9
寒	寒	hán	cold	7
漢	汉	hàn	man	10
航	航	háng	to navigate	3
合	合	hé	to combine	1
乎	乎	hū	(a particle expressing doubt or conjecture)	4
胡	胡	hú	barbarian, (胡琴: two-string bow instrument)	2
戶	户	hù	door; (bank) account	6
花	花	huā	(of eyes) blurred	4
畫	画	huà	to draw, paint	2
化	化	huà	變化: change	3
壞	坏	huài	bad	1
換	换	huàn	to exchange	6
匯	汇	huì	collection	6

J

及	及	jí	to reach, attain	7
己	己	jǐ	oneself	2
繫	系	jì	to fasten	3
計	计	jì	to count, calculate	3
季	季	jì	season	7
寄	寄	jì	to mail, send	6
技	技	jì	skill	8
價	价	jià	price, value	8
堅	坚	jiān	hard, firm	9
減	减	jiǎn	to reduce	9
降	降	jiàng	to fall, lower	3
交	交	jiāo	(of places or periods of time) meet, join	3
街	街	jiē	street	4
節	节	jié	part; festival	8
界	界	jiè	boundary	5
津	津	jīn	saliva	5
金	金	jīn	gold	6
精	精	jīng	energy, spirit	4
睛	睛	jīng	eyeball	4
鏡	镜	jìng	mirror	1
俱	俱	jù	all, completely	4
聚	聚	jù	to gather	4
據	据	jù	to depend on	10

K

卡	卡	kǎ	card	6
康	康	kāng	healthy	4
控	控	kòng	to control	9
口	口	kǒu	mouth, entrance	3
款	款	kuǎn	a sum of money	6
睏	困	kùn	sleepy	4

L

拉	拉	lā	to play (certain musical instruments)	2
累	累	lèi	tired	1

李	李	lǐ	行李: luggage	1
理	理	lǐ	to put in order	1
里	里	lǐ	公里: kilometer	3
利	利	lì	profit, interest	6
歷	历	lì	to go through	8
連	连	lián	even	8
臉	脸	liǎn	face	2
涼	凉	liáng	cool, cold	4
零	零	líng	zero	10
靈	灵	líng	quick, clever	9
落	落	luò	to drop, land	3
率	率	lǜ	rate	6

M

滿	满	mǎn	full	2
描	描	miáo	to copy, retouch	8
苗	苗	miáo	苗條: slim	9
民	民	mín	people	3
末	末	mò	end	8
母	母	mǔ	mother	4
慕	慕	mù	to admire, yarn for	7

N

拿	拿	ná	to hold	2
鬧	闹	nào	to do, make	5
農	农	nóng	agriculture	3

O

喔	喔	ō	(an interjection indicating sudden realization)	3

P

爬	爬	pá	to climb	10
片	片	piàn	thin piece	2
品	品	pǐn	article, product	3
破	破	pò	broken	1

Q

戚	戚	qī	relative	7
器	器	qì	utensil, ware	2
千	千	qiān	thousand	6
簽	签	qiān	to sign, label	7
牆	墙	qiáng	wall	2
強	强	qiáng	strong; better	8
且	且	qiě	而且: also, in addition	8
親	亲	qīn	relative	7
琴	琴	qín	a general name mostly for string instruments	2
輕	轻	qīng	small in degree	4
情	情	qíng	affection	5
曲	曲	qū	bend, crooked	10
取	取	qǔ	to take, withdraw	6
趣	趣	qù	interest	8
全	全	quán	whole; intact	3

R

榮	荣	róng	glory	5

S

掃	扫	sǎo	to sweep	1
廈	厦	shà	tall building	5
山	山	shān	mountain	3
商	商	shāng	trade, business	10
社	社	shè	agency, society	7
神	神	shén	spirit	2
食	食	shí	food	9
史	史	shǐ	history	8
適	适	shì	fit, suitable	4
瘦	瘦	shòu	thin	9
受	受	shòu	to receive	10
樹	树	shù	tree	1
數	数	shù	number	7
死	死	sǐ	dead	1
鬆	松	sōng	loose, slack	8
素	素	sù	basic element	4
訴	诉	sù	to tell	10
算	算	suàn	to plan, calculate	3
雖	虽	suī	although	5

T

它	它	tā	it	8
台	台	tái	stage, platform	2
彈	弹	tán	to play (a musical instrument), pluck	2
套	套	tào	cover	1
特	特	tè	specially	4
填	填	tián	to fill in	6
甜	甜	tián	sweet	9
田	田	tián	field	3
挺	挺	tǐng	very, quite	5
團	团	tuán	group	5

W

彎	弯	wān	curve	3
完	完	wán	finish, complete	8
往	往	wǎng	to, towards	3
忘	忘	wàng	to forget	1
望	望	wàng	to hope	10
維	维	wéi	to maintain	4
味	味	wèi	taste	4
誤	误	wù	to miss	5

X

希	希	xī	to hope	10
戲	戏	xì	traditional Chinese opera	2
羨	羡	xiàn	to admire, envy	7
箱	箱	xiāng	box, case	1
香	香	xiāng	aroma, good smell	4
相	相	xiāng	mutually	4
向	向	xiàng	to, towards	3
笑	笑	xiào	to laugh	5
效	效	xiào	effect	8
需	需	xū	need	9
蓄	蓄	xù	to save up	6
旬	旬	xún	a period of ten days	10

Y

呀	呀	ya	(indicating surprise)	1
顏	颜	yán	color	8
演	演	yǎn	to perform, play	2
眼	眼	yǎn	eye	4
衣	衣	yī	clothes	1
宜	宜	yí	suitable	7
亦	亦	yì	also	4
陰	阴	yīn	overcast	5
銀	银	yín	silver	6
引	引	yǐn	to lead, attract	8
飲	饮	yǐn	drink	9
永	永	yǒng	forever	4
遊	游	yóu	to wander about	7
右	右	yòu	right	3
於	于	yú	終於: at last	5
原	原	yuán	primary, original	7
元	元	yuán	dollar	6
越	越	yuè	to exceed	9

Z

載	载	zài	to carry, be loaded with	10
咱	咱	zán	we (including both the speaker and the person/s spoken to)	1
早	早	zǎo	early	9
責	责	zé	duty	1
展	展	zhǎn	to stretch	3
站	站	zhàn	to stand	2
帳	账	zhàng	account	6
照	照	zhào	to take (pictures)	2
著	着	zhe	(a particle indicating an aspect)	2
折	折	zhé	to bend, twist	10
整	整	zhěng	to put in order	1
證	证	zhèng	certificate	7
之	之	zhī	(a particle)	6
支	支	zhī	to pay out; withdraw	6
職	职	zhí	duty	6
值	值	zhí	to be worth	5
直	直	zhí	straight	3
制	制	zhì	to control	9
終	终	zhōng	end	5
種	种	zhǒng	kind, type	2
眾	众	zhòng	multitude	2
週	周	zhōu	week; circuit	8

Name: ____________________ Date: ______________

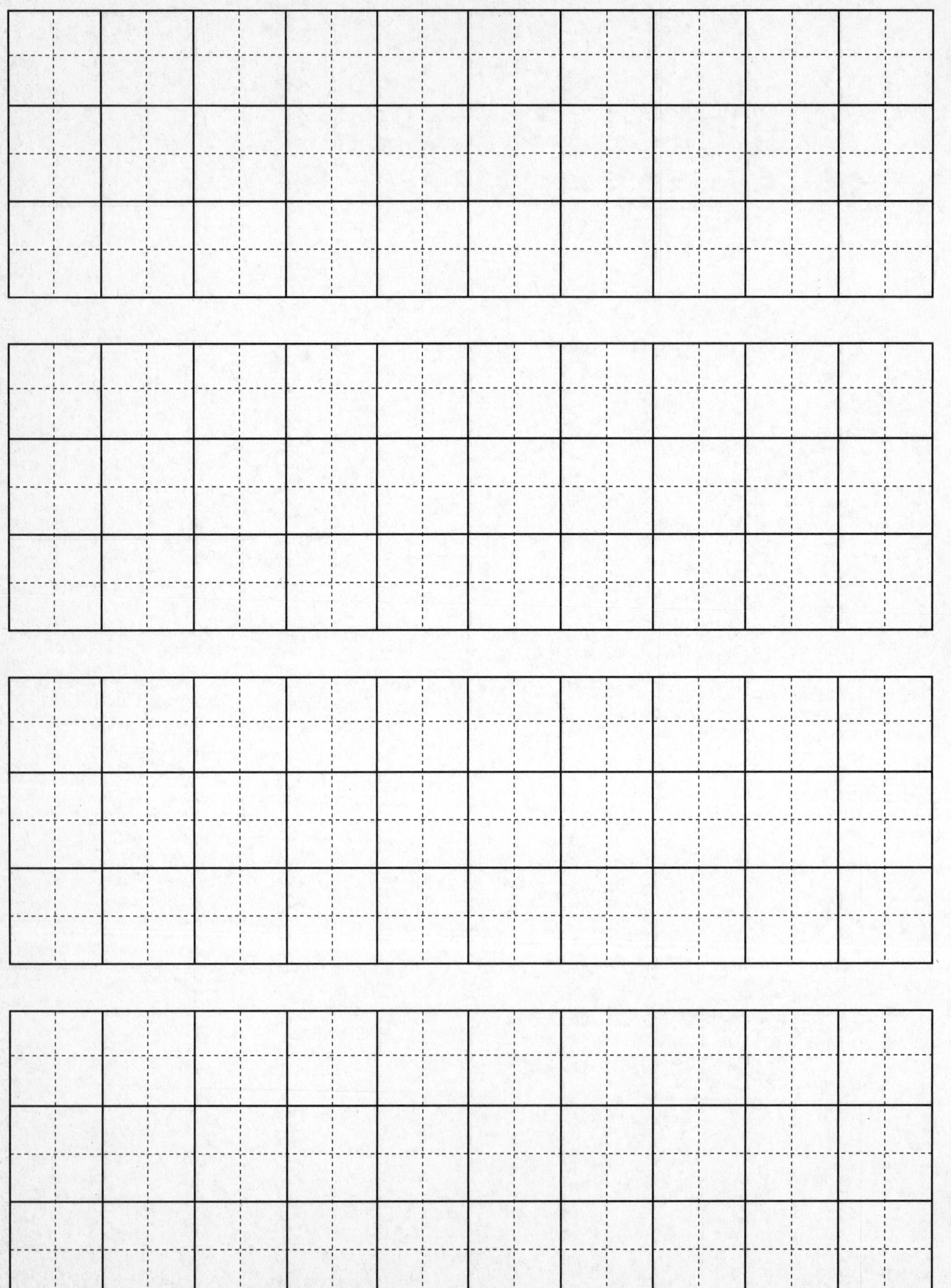